Dear Diana —
Good luck with
your horrifying decision.
and get some dogs —
love
Muriel

A

Merrill Markoe's Guide to Love

ALSO BY MERRILL MARKOE

How to Be Hap-Hap-Happy Like Me

What the Dogs Have Taught Me

Merrill Markoe's Guide to Love

by Merrill Markoe

Atlantic Monthly Press

NEW YORK

The following selections were previously published, in a different form, in *New Woman*: "Why Can't a Woman Have Sex Like a Man?," "Secretz of Seduction," "Looking for Love in All the Wrong Places," "Learning to Live a Lie," "The Pet Psychic Cometh," and "What the Movies Taught Me."

Published simultaneously in Canada
Printed in the United States of America

FIRST EDITION

Library of Congress Cataloging-in-Publication Data

Markoe, Merrill.
    Merrill Markoe's guide to Love / by Merrill Markoe.
        p.   cm.
    ISBN 0-87113-663-5
    1. Man-woman relationships.   2. Man-woman relationships—Humor.
3. Love.   4. Love—Humor.
HQ801.M3714   1997
306.7—dc21   96-39605

Design by Laura Hammond Hough

Atlantic Monthly Press
841 Broadway
New York, NY 10003

10 9 8 7 6 5 4 3 2 1

I WOULD LIKE TO THANK RUTH WORKMAN, LEWIS, BO, TEX AND Winky, Kristine McKenna, Polly Draper, Michael Wolff, Nat Wolff, Margy Rochlin, Larry Dean, Judy Chen, Deborah Price, Stella Kleinrock, Mavis Leno, Carol Gary, Rosanna Arquette, Chrissie Hynde, Seane Corn, The Learning Annex, Vanilla Ice, Cynthia Heimel, Beth Lapides, Gregory Miller, Jennifer Grey, my brother Glenn, and my friend Christine.

Thanks also to Melanie Jackson, Carla Lalli, and Morgan Entrekin.

Contents

Foreword   I

1. What Is Love: A Very Broad Overview   5

2. What Causes Love?   15

3. The Beginning—Early Signs of Interest: The Good, the Bad, and the Terrifying   19

4. How to Become Irresistible to the Opposite Sex   27

5. Why Can't a Woman Have Sex Like a Man?   35

6. Man into Putty   39

7. Secretz of Seduction   47

8. Speed Seduction: The Cliff Notes   57

9. Dating Phase Two?   65

10. Finding Your Perfect Mate   69

11.   *Tips on Dating a Crazy Person*   83

12.   *Warped Perspective: Love and Sex on the Astral Plane*   89

13.   *Looking for Love in All the Wrong Places*   97

14.   *Learning to Live a Lie*   107

15.   *Looking Forward to Disappointment*   115

16.   *Getting To I Do*   123

17.   *Animal Love*   131

18.   *The Pet Psychic Cometh*   141

19.   *Marriage: What the Hell Is Going On Exactly?*   147

20.   *What the Movies Taught Me*   161

21.   *Divine Love*   167

22.   *A Wrap-Up*   173

Foreword

I HAVE HAD PRETTY BAD LUCK IN LOVE. BUT AT LEAST I FIND MYSELF in good company. Most of the people I know have had pretty bad luck in love too.

In fact, these days when I see an authentic happy couple, I try to stand very, very still so I don't scare them away . . . and then I study their every move as carefully as I can to try and see what makes them tick, not unlike the way Margaret Mead used to do with the Trobriand Islanders.

It doesn't seem fair to blame my lack of success in love on my early influences. Who *doesn't* use that excuse these days? Plus, I don't know anyone whose parents provided them with a reasonable relationship model.

Like a lot of people of their generation, my parents thought of family life as a safe haven for misery. They bickered endlessly. They usually appeared to be exasperated to the point of barely tolerating each other. Yet if you asked them about it, they would be happy to talk on and on about what a happy fulfilling marriage they had. So I grew up believing that rage and exasperation were love's most appropriate expressions. And fortunately for me, I was able to find many ways to make this very kind of love materialize in my own life.

My parents didn't seem to have much other advice to share on the topic of love. They did, however, view each and every potential love candidate of mine as though they were scrutinizing a police artist's sketch of a suspect. "Officer, I don't think that's him," their frozen faces would say.

But they were skeptical people. In fact, my father was the founder of a religious sect known as Negative Zen, best described by his most commonly repeated mantra: "Let's *go* so we can get *back*."

Not too surprisingly, all my instincts regarding the matter of love were skewed and unreliable from the very beginning, as an entry from my fifth-grade diary, describing my earliest known flirtation with a member of the opposite sex, clearly describes. The incident occurred on a Thursday in May when at the age of eleven I attempted to intrigue a boy on whom I had a huge crush.

"I drew a picture on a piece of paper," I wrote in that big, round handwriting that is mandatory for girls that age, "and I said, 'To Wayne. Roses are Red, Violets are Blue, I killed my dog 'cause he looked like you,' and then I left it on his bicycle." "I wonder if he got it?" I mused wistfully at the bottom of the page, not comprehending for the first of what would go on to be thousands and thousands of times to come that sarcasm is *not* an effective tool of seduction. I was even dumber in college than I was in grade school, if such a thing is possible. Once I no longer had my parents' authority to answer to, my own approach to love and relationships became simple: When I met a guy I kind of liked, I would follow him toward a cup of coffee. And if that seemed to go pretty well, I would live with him for three years.

In fact, it is only recently that I figured out that you do not have to live with someone on the first date.

Which brings me to my present quandary: In the court records that are my life, I have not a shred of proof that I have ever done anything right in the game of love.

But while more primitive, less complicated societies provide rituals and traditions to guide the confused, the astronomical divorce rate even among the village elders in our culture has left all us garden-variety love chumps rudderless and without logical leaders. And under the clear impression that there is *no one sane* to ask what we should do next.

But then it occurred to me—Hey!—I am a resident of Los Angeles, a city that has a wide variety of experts on tap to address every need. No city is more devoted to the idea of self-improvement.

And once I began to look, I had not the slightest amount of trouble finding dozens of classes, seminars, and weekend retreats being held continuously to address every conceivable love dilemma. I saw notices for them in catalogs and posted in supermarkets and coffeehouses. I found flyers stacked on the floors of drugstores and taped to the sides of cappuccino machines. They appeared via direct mail right to my very door. And I soon learned that all over the city, in conference rooms, restaurants, classrooms, hotels suites, libraries, houses of worship, etc., groups of people were assembling to discuss all aspects of love.

It's true that I would never have attended even one of these meetings were I not writing a book. But I was kind of curious to hear what they had to say. Maybe, I thought to myself, if I did some real research, I could uncover a few strategies that have eluded me. Maybe there *are* people who have an enlightened message to share. And if they do exist, I had better get to them immediately—before they become too involved in divorce litigation to have time to talk.

What follows here are the results of my semi-inexhaustible efforts to consume every piece of advice on the topic of love that crossed my path. And when I use the word *every*, I use it, of course, in the traditional journalistic sense meaning "a couple here and there, when it was convenient."

I invite you to join me, now, on a slide show of my journey.

Chapter 1
What Is Love: A Very Broad Overview

IT SEEMS LIKE THE WHOLE WORLD IS OBSESSED WITH LOVE, ALTHOUGH no one can really agree what it actually *is*. No one can really agree about the definition of a black hole in space or the origin of the universe, yet you don't catch hundreds of people trying to write a song about either of those.

For some reason, where love is concerned, ignorance and confusion are not a handicap to being considered an expert.

For a thing we really can't identify, we are all certainly very preoccupied with finding it, keeping it, maintaining it, reviving it, getting rid of it, and then starting it all over again anew. People yearn for love. They beg and weep and whimper for love. Until an actual human being comes into their life and wants something from them. Then they weep and whine and groan about how much love hurts and how messed up they are now and how much better off they were alone. It is similar to a dog's relationship to the car. First they cry because they want to get *in* to the car. Then, as soon as the car starts to move, they cry because they want to get *out*. And of course, as soon as they get out, all they want to do is get back in as soon as possible. Good thing for us, dogs aren't especially musical or just imagine all the annoying songs there'd be about cars.

Apparently, there are ten thousand song titles on file at the U.S. Copyright Office starting with the words "Love is." Among them:

"Love Is a Shoogy Shoo" (1912) and "Love Is a Dimpling Doodle Bug" (1943). Like all theories about love, these are hard to dispute. Even the official definition of love is ever changing. In 1957, *Webster's Encyclopedia Dictionary* defined love as "a strong deep attachment, great affection, especially for one of the opposite sex." Below that it says, "Love affair: the condition of mutual love between members of the opposite sex." Below that it says, "Love apple: the fruit of the tomato plant."

Aside from the fact that gay love is totally overlooked by these definitions, as are affectionate relationships among family members, same-sex friends, and people and their animals, there is an even greater outrage. I was only a kid in 1957, but I was certainly old enough to know that even in those less sophisticated times, *no one* was going around calling tomatoes love apples.

(Just one more compelling reason to write this book, so that if sometime in the far future archeologists are digging through the rubble of our destroyed civilization and decide to re-create 1957 for a museum diorama by depicting a mother making a salad out of lettuce, carrots, cucumbers, and love apples, they will know the truth. People of the future take note: It was tomatoes in 1957. And it has been for the whole century pretty much.) Happily, by 1994 Webster's had updated its definition of love to read: "an intense, affectionate concern for or passionate attraction to another person," which though more politically correct (although it still leaves out animals), is actually less of a working definition for women than it is for men.

Especially when you consider that many women spend a great deal of their lives trying to comprehend the *difference* between a passionate attraction and love: a distinction that is not nearly so difficult for men to make, because, of course, they invented it.

Just for the record, the difference is this: If what appears to be a passionate attraction is able to sustain itself for at least a year, then it can be correctly defined as love, even if by that point both people actively hate each other.

The Poets Try to Help

There are a million approaches to being in love. A brief perusal of Bartlett's *Familiar Quotations* reveals an almost endless supply of poetic and philosophical takes on the subject. For instance, when the poet Sir John Suckling (his real name; 1609–1642) wrote:

> *Why so pale and wan, fond lover*
> *Prithee why so pale*
> *Will when looking well can't move her*
> *Looking ill prevail*

we hear a poet sharing the kind of brilliant strategy that could only have been devised by a man who, after all, was dead by the age of thirty-three. In the classic manner of getting lemons and making lemonade, Sir John Suckling taps in to the rich tradition of using physical ailments as a manipulative springboard to love.

The book/movie *Love Story* explains a version of this same approach with the poetic thought "Love means never having to say you're sorry." Even though it has certainly been my experience that love means having to say you're sorry *over and over and over.*

For a true poetic overview of the current cultural climate of love, one need look no further than the combined oeuvre of America's most beloved pantheon of writers—the poets of Hallmark.

For example, the Hallmark poet Renee Duvall gives a voice to the tortured obsessive-compulsive lover in this poem from the current "Between You and Me" series:

> *Every song on the radio*
> *seems to be about love,*
> *and I miss you.*
> *Every time my phone rings*
> *and I hear*
> *someone else's voice,*
> *I miss you.*

Here, Duvall attempts to explain how it feels to be a lover with a tenuous link to reality. As does the Hallmark poem "Love Means So Many Things" (Anon.) in which a distressed lover speaks of a terrifying tumble into the abyss:

It means trusting myself with someone
Who has seen me at my worst . . .
It means teasing each other and laughing
at inside jokes that nobody but us understands.

The reader is left to imagine what rages and delusional behaviors "my worst" might refer to as the confusion and panic that result from losing the ability to communicate with the outside world begin to escalate. An even more nightmarish struggle in the face of a disintegrating mental, emotional, and sociocultural landscape is poignantly detailed in this chilling anonymously written Hallmark first-person account of someone in the throes of a bipolar disorder:

There are times when I'm moody,
and, no matter what you do or say,
I'll find fault.
I know that, at times, I push you
to the point where you feel that
You just can't win,
and you wonder what you
could possibly be doing wrong . . .
Well, it's not you, it's me.

To further underline the dark sense of isolation experienced by the mentally ill, the verse is eerily accompanied by a tiny charcoal drawing of a western landscape where we see a little picket fence stretching out over a receding hillside.

The anonymous poet goes on to request that his lover become as lost in delusional thinking as he is, and ends with a frightening murder-suicide threat:

I know it's no excuse,
but those times
when I'm the most difficult
are probably the times
I'm loving you the most
and I can't bear the thought
of life without you.

The Hallmark love poet Alarie Tennille goes even further into this dark terrain with a poem that alludes to the kind of memory lapses that may indicate multiple personality disorder.

It's hard to remember
to tell you how much
I love you,
especially when I'm
all stressed out.

This desperate cry for help is subtly underscored by a typically spooky Hallmark photograph of a vine of roses—

The insane, unstable, and terrifying love described by the Hallmark Poets threads them to the rich tapestry of mentally disabled love poets throughout the history of literature. It has long been the domain of poets to cloak love-addled mental problems in such an impressive display of verbal pyrotechnics that regular people can't easily tell just how completely nuts they really were.

Tragic flaws and peculiar perspectives aside, the great poets have forever influenced the way love and sex are viewed by the masses. Consider, for instance, the wide-reaching influence of Elizabeth

Barrett Browning's poem "How Do I Love Thee, Let Me Count the Ways."

It is certainly the poetic ancestor of the current book "203 Ways to Drive a Man Wild in Bed," a book I purchased because I was intrigued by the number 203. Never having taken a personal inventory or any kind of a survey among my friends, I didn't really know how many driving-man-wild ways the average woman already has in her arsenal. But I think that if I had made a list and gotten to, say, 80, 90 ways, I would have thought "Hell, that's *plenty* of ways" and been so overcome with self-congratulations that I would have called it a day and taken everyone I know out for a beer.

And what *were* author–love poet Olivia St. Clare's 203 (let us count them) ways? Well, the depth, the breadth, and the height of the soul were not among them. And just a few of them were a teensy bit obvious. For example, #25: "Play sensuous background music." Who hasn't thought of that? (Currently, I use a tape of Offspring singing "Low Self-Esteem.") Number 34 was more perplexing: "How pleasantly surprised he'll be when you attack him in your very own bushes." Now I know I'm being literal-minded here, but the title of the book *is* "203 ways to drive a man wild *in bed*," so if she means for us to drag the damn bed all the way outside into the bushes, she is naively overlooking the fact that nothing is less conducive to an erotic experience than a branch in the wrong place. With the possible exception of sand.

And then there's suggestion #18, in which we are told that "the musky perfume of your own natural lubricant can make an incredible aphrodisiac. . . . Before you see your man, try using some of your own cassolette [sic] as you would your favorite perfume: a touch behind the ears, at the throat. . . ." Even supposing one would be willing to attempt this somewhat risky behavior, mightn't the gnats and flies that would be attracted by the "perfume" tend to contraindicate the benefits?

In fact, many of the 203 suggestions wouldn't work at all. For instance #8: "Tape record your love-making session." I am thinking now of a particular guy I knew who always insisted on leaving the television on. A tape recording of one of *those* sessions played back might have consisted of the faint rustling of sheets and the lilting voice of Conan O'Brien.

Then again, some of the suggestions are sure-fire. Like #74: "Costume yourself as a nurse . . . or a circus performer." I have yet to meet the man whose pulse didn't quicken at the sight of a woman in those really big clown shoes.

Longfellow said, "If I am not worth the wooing, I am not worth the winning." This may be true. But having scoured this book on wooing, I am afraid I was forced to conclude that the author arrived at 203 ways because she was getting paid by the way.

Still More Confusion

For an even more thorough cataloging of the time-honored mixup concerning sex and love, a person really need look no further than the classic Sanskrit text, the Kama-sutra. Dated between 1 and 6 A.D., it proves beyond a doubt just how long people have been swirling in a whirlpool of craziness on this topic, hoping desperately that if they organize their thoughts into neat little lists perhaps they will eventually seem to make sense.

Among other things, the Kama-sutra explains how "sexual intercourse can be compared to a quarrel, on account of the contrarieties of love and its tendency to dispute." It recommends "striking" as a love staple, delineating four classic techniques:

- striking with the back of the hand
- striking with the fingers a little contracted
- striking with the fist
- striking with the open palm of the hand

Nowadays we call this kind of love domestic abuse. But I guess what differentiates Kama-sutra–style striking from the kind we see on every episode of "Cops" are the sounds that the Kama-sutra recommends as proper accompaniment. Domestic abuse is often punctuated by sounds like "*Help!*" and "*Go fuck yourself*"; the Kama-sutra's love sounds are:

The sound HIN
The thundering sound
The cooing sound
The weeping sound
The sound PHUT
The sound PHAT
The sound SUT
The sound PLAT

Some of these sounds are rarely used anymore. Many people in today's busy world have difficulty figuring out how to effectively employ the sound PHUT or the sound PLAT without destroying the mood. But the sound PHAT and the weeping sound still certainly go hand and hand. Perhaps these days more than ever.

As the Kama-sutra tells us, "When the man, making the sound PHAT, strikes the woman on the head with the fingers of his hand a little contracted, it is called Prasritaka, which means striking with the fingers of the hand a little contracted." Certainly as good a reason for naming a thing as any I've heard. But also an important reminder that weight gain has been a source of tension in love relationships for a very long time.

Of course, for sheer originality in the Confusion-of-Love-and-Sex sweepstakes, no one can hold a candle to the Taoists, as they are happy to prove page after page in the book *Taoist Secrets of Love*.

The real substance of the book is presented in the chapter entitled "Semen Retention." This refers to a method of orgasm the

Taoists endorse that avoids ejaculation because "the loss of semen by any means causes the life span to be shortened." (Well, that is certainly true for the life span of any potential Taoist offspring.)

But why do this? The Taoists feel it is possible for a man to save up this energy, recycle it, and thereby generate creative and healing energy for his use alone—probably not a bad idea, since "alone" is the condition in which he may find himself, considering how grouchy he will become if he persists in this practice.

"The power which you have begun to generate with the retention of the seed is enormous," the book goes on. "It has the force to crack massive bone. . . . For this reason the suture atop the skull of advanced adepts often loosens. The power can drill through plates of the skull, increasing cranial capacity and opening direct access to higher energies."

Higher energies aside, when one considers how goofy men behave simply from too much testosterone, one has to wonder about the wisdom of associating with any who also have a loosened skull. And while perhaps this does offer an explanation for the behavior of self-proclaimed practitioner Woody Harrelson, it also amounts to a very good reason to bring along the pepper spray on a date with a Taoist.

As it turns out, love is just a big biochemical bouillabaisse. Testosterone is only one ingredient. And as is the case with any bouillabaisse, especially in this the age of ebola and E. coli, it is a good idea to find out what all those hard-to-identify floating ingredients are before you consume too much of them.

Chapter 2
What Causes Love?

BIOLOGICALLY SPEAKING, LOVE IS AS PECULIAR A MIX OF BIZARRE chemicals as any fat-free frozen-dinner entrée.

First of all, there is a chemical called *Oxytocin*, which causes feelings of bonding with a love object. Not too surprisingly, it turns out that women produce about fifty times more of this during sex than do men. Which certainly explains a lot.

Then there are pheromones—chemical substances that all people produce that amount to our personal "smell prints."

Historically, scent has always played a big role in love. Napoleon reportedly sent a letter to Josephine saying, "I will be arriving in Paris tomorrow. Don't wash." Not too surprisingly, there is no record of Josephine having returned the compliment.

Human sexual pheromones apparently create a chemical sense of well-being and inexplicable feelings of intimacy in us, even with a relative stranger.

Considering that this is the way love begins, it actually makes pretty good sense that a torrent of confusion is where it often all ends.

How Long Does Romantic Love Last?

Scientists tell us that from "the moment of infatuation to when a feeling of neutrality for one's love object sets in" typically takes from eighteen months to three years.

Obviously, this varies from person to person, as we see in Charlie Sheen, for whom the entire process takes between two and six hours.

But apparently for most of us there is a chemical explanation. The brain can't maintain the revved-up status that results from producing the chemical PEA (phenylethylamine), which is very similar to speed. So the brain first stops reacting to it and then stops producing it.

I believe this PEA is probably the same chemical that creates the impulse to continually change the TV channel. Which is why, on the bright side, as romantic love dies, couples begin to actually watch an entire program more often.

Now an even more potentially dangerous emotional situation emerges: ATTACHMENT.

And once again the difference turns out to be chemical. In this phase, when the lovers are in each other's company, the production of *endorphins* is stimulated. Endorphins calm the mind, kill pain, and reduce anxiety. Aerobic exercise such as running also produces endorphins. Perhaps this is the reason that so many people, at about the three-year mark, decide to start running and just keep on going.

I have a theory that has yet to be proved or even tested by science. I suspect that what we call love may be an allergic reaction. I have read studies that prove that an allergic person may be *attracted* to the very things to which they are *allergic*. And as with more traditional allergies, the victims (or lovers) cause each other to suffer from a range of symptoms such as chills, dizziness, queasy stomach, anxiety, hives.

We all know that statistically the average love affair is destined to unravel. And now we know that the absence of PEA may be one cause. So perhaps the love affairs that prevail despite these overwhelming odds and multiple symptoms succeed because the people involved have developed allergic antibodies to each other.

If this underresearched theory of mine is true, then the only way a person could tell the difference between a traditional allergy (say to cornstarch) and LOVE is that when it is a regular allergy, the parties involved are much less likely to be institutionalized, commit murder, or be arrested for stalking. In other words, if you find yourself compulsively checking the answering machine all day long and are concerned you are losing your mind, it is probably not a traditional food allergy that is bothering you.

There is another, even more insidious element at the core of the behavior we call love. It is what psychologists call "repetition compulsion." This is a phenomenon that amounts to the compelling desire by people to re-create for themselves the most familiar situation from their childhoods. Not the *best* one, mind you. It doesn't even have to have been pleasant. It just has to have been frequent and familiar. It's the old "I want a girl just like the girl that married dear old Dad" thing. This is fine if the girl who married dear old Dad was a reasonable, loving person. But many people have (or did have) narcissistic, negative, complicated, even sado-masochistic people for parents. And I mean that in the nicest way possible. Maybe they were not even knowingly nuts—just too primitive to make any sense or stop being a constant pain in the ass.

The children of such parents wind up with unconscious emotional radar that is able to seek out and find other people who will supply them with a duplicate of this very situation in spades.

God and the Universe have plotted to make life completely untenable for them by arranging to resubmit a version of these very same screwed-up people *repackaged* as an irresistible member of the sex to which they are attracted. It is just like watching *Invasion of the Body Snatchers,* only with reduced inclination to purchase Raisinettes. Here is a person who seems to have nothing at all in common with the parent that caused you grief—I mean, how can you even imagine that this twenty-four-year-old bikini model has anything in common with your seventy-four-year-old former steel-worker father? Ha! But guess what? That's exactly what has happened. Your unconscious is able to miraculously function like a heat-seeking missile to search out and locate a person to whom you will be *very attracted* who does in fact duplicate the most impossible, the most preposterous, the most totally screwed-up traits of either one or both of your parents.

Say you grew up with a mother who was so controlling and overbearing, so domineering and manipulative that you have no choice except to stop speaking to her entirely. Your unconscious will not rest until it is able to find for you a beautiful supermodel or a handsome, brilliant, talented man who appears to totally adore you but in time will reveal her or himself to be so controlling and manipulative, so overbearing and domineering that you will have no choice except to stop speaking to them entirely. They will turn out to be so exactly like your mother that you might as well buy them a Mother's Day card.

This is what is at the core of LOVE AT FIRST SIGHT. It is when your heat-seeking unconscious finds its hoped-for, truly screwed-up target. It's the only frightening, unavoidable catastrophe that thousands of people write songs and poems about each year.

The only hope you have of escaping this dilemma is if: 1) you had a parent you *liked,* or 2) your repackaged parent clone turns out by some miraculous twist of fate to be interested in growth and change—an option that is a greater statistical rarity than the odds of winning a lottery. Particularly for women, since in my experience getting a man to go to therapy is similar to trying to talk a cat into going for a swim.

There *is* a solution to this dilemma, but so far therapists have resisted my suggestion that they find some way to keep score every session or at the very least consider offering a point spread.

Maybe one day.

Chapter 3
The Beginning—Early Signs of Interest: The Good, the Bad, and the Terrifying

LOVE USUALLY BEGINS WITH FLIRTATION.

Traditionally, flirtation is that period in which initial attraction causes people to act giddy and way too nice to each other. It is important to identify this and begin to enjoy it as quickly as possible because in many cases it is the only phase of the relationship during which you will be able to talk the other person into doing certain kinds of things. For instance, it is the only time I can get a guy to pull off the road and stop at Santa Claus Lane to see what they have for sale in the off-season.

Psychotherapist Pat Allen says that making eye contact is key to success in flirtation, and that for casual eye contact to have the necessary emotional charge to register as flirtatious it must last two seconds longer than random eye contact—or five seconds in total.

It is a good idea to learn how to tell the difference between a flirtatious five-second eye hit and the early moments of a psychotic stare. My rule of thumb is this: If the person who is making eye contact with you for five seconds or longer also has visible beads of perspiration accumulating on any portion of their anatomy, forget about giving them your phone number.

There are other behaviors that people commonly exhibit when they flirt. Sociologists have noticed that people's voices become more sing-songy. This is because in flirting, *form* supersedes content. In other words, the *way* that people say things has more impact than *what* they are actually saying.[1] Desmond Morris calls this *grooming talk*.

However, I have found that it is a big mistake not to listen very carefully to what passes for content during this flirtation phase because there is often greater honesty in this unprotected state. There is less at stake. Sometimes a simple answering-machine message can reveal an entire microcosm of what the relationship will eventually become. You will need to learn to decode what is said. For instance, what follows is the transcript of an actual answering-machine message I received from a guy I had met only once at a party:

HIM: "I'd like to see you sometime, the earlier the better. Right now would be perfect. If you're in the mood to do something tonight, that would be good because my moods shift so dramatically these days that it's easier for me to go on impulse than to make a date with someone and then realize when the time comes that I am not really in the mood to do anything. So that's kind of the way I want to operate."

And he didn't use a sing-songy voice, either. If this is what a person gets out for "grooming talk," you are in big trouble when they think the bloom is off the rose.

Other mannerisms associated with flirting are "a smile, a coy look, a head toss, a chest thrust, and a gaze," says one anthropologist. A flirting male will make a big deal out of a simple gesture such as lighting a cigarette.[2]

---

[1]This is also true in show business. The main difference being that in show business there is rarely *any* eye contact and there is also far more kissing.

[2]If you live in Los Angeles these same behaviors can indicate that you are with an actor or actress who has spotted a potential employer and is hoping to showcase themselves for a possible job, in which case they may not be remotely interested in you. (See Chapter 11, "Tips on Dating a Crazy Person.") Which, believe me, is for the best.

I myself have been known to be truly terrible at the aforementioned. If I toss my head and thrust my chest, I stand a good chance of knocking something over. So my version of flirting is to sit very, very still and try not to spill anything on myself. In an ideal world I would then distribute a small printed card not unlike the ones I have received from deaf people at airports. Only mine would say, "I am flirting impaired. You may not know this, but I am flirting with you." If the object of my advances offered me a small donation, I would call it a hit and give him my phone number. This would, with any luck, lead to:

Dating Phase One

When I was the age at which people usually date, I never really dated.

You have to take into account that I was at UC Berkeley at the tail end of the sixties and the early part of the seventies, when you were required to present a good, strong, rational explanation for why you did *not* want to sleep with someone who had been the least bit nice to you. I remember one guy who came up to me on the student union steps, where I was bending down to greet a friendly dog. He wanted to know why I would be so free with my affections for a strange dog and not extend him the same courtesy. And I remember momentarily considering this philosophical conundrum like it was something I needed to ponder. Of course, now I know that the appropriate response would have been: "Because (a) at least the *dog* appears to be relatively free of sucking parasites and mange, and (b) because you are a big fucking asshole."

So I came late to the information that dating is the process by which two people who have a certain attraction to each other decide whether they like each other enough to proceed to "torturous pseudo-love hell."

What Is Dating?

Dating is an *evaluation* period, usually involving a meal and, in about 75 percent of first dates, also a movie. This is why so many Hollywood movies are violent and simplistic: They are assembled by men who date a lot and are just trying to subliminally prepare the women who interest them for the reality of a relationship with them, should it come to that.

Men and women tend to have different first-date agendas. Women are mainly scrutinizing and assessing a guy with an eye toward his potential in a long-term relationship. Is he smart? Is he annoying? How annoying? *Real* annoying or the kind of "somewhat annoying" they think they'll be able to change. The woman is trolling for *sparks*. She is hoping for *chemistry*. But the strangest little things can wreck this for her.

I recently talked to a woman who turned off to a guy she kind of liked because "he had a really weak stride" when he walked. Another woman I know couldn't take a guy seriously after she noticed that he had had a manicure. And while these judgments may appear to be petty and superficial, they are also critical to the woman because she knows they may be the last ones she ever gets to make. Because if things move forward and she ends up sleeping with the guy, and the oxytocin, the pheromones, and the PEA kick in, he will be able to show up dead drunk at four in the morning dressed in a mattress cover and a porkpie hat screaming foul epithets and threatening to strangle her with a garden hose and she will still not be sure she should throw him out because now she feels she "loves" him.

An important mistake that women make is assuming that men are dating for the same reason they are. Which is why a woman usually puts way too much thought into figuring out what to wear. Some women will change five or six times before they arrive at what they think is the right combination of "alluring yet assertive," "fashionable and at the same time individualistic," "sexy but not necessarily compliant."

Men do not put this kind of thought into the first-date wardrobe because they have already done all the evaluating they need to before this point. That they agreed to the date at all explains their whole agenda. By agreeing to go on the date in the first place, the man has also already said yes to the possibility of sex. He probably sees dinner and the movie as two necessary stalling tactics. Unless the movie involves some kind of martial arts, in which case he was probably going to see it anyway. Which is why many men's idea of the appropriate attire, no matter what the occasion, is jeans, a T-shirt, and an article of clothing that is associated with a team sport, an individual sport or an organization with manly cultural implications. Like, say, a baseball jacket, a fisherman's vest, and a fireman's helmet—or a motorcycle jacket, a baseball cap, and cowboy boots. Okay—I've never seen anyone on a date wearing a fireman's helmet, but my life is not over yet and I expect to.

Maybe men do this because they do not want to appear to be trying too hard. Maybe they also feel insecure and get added confidence by identifying themselves with something indisputably male. Or maybe it was the only thing they owned that wasn't wedged under the bed or between the bed and the wall and was not covered with clumps of hair.

The net result is two people, seated side by side in a car, who appear to be headed for two different destinations. This sets the tone for much of what is to come should this particular bus actually leave the depot. She is wearing something she saw in *Vogue,* and he has on a flak jacket and waders. These mismatched signals will continue until someone's head explodes. If the exploding head belongs to the woman, she will find herself in therapy, where she will learn that it is possible for forty-five minutes to be called an hour. She will be told that no, she is not crazy. The situation she finds herself in is "crazy making."

If the exploding head belongs to the man, he has several additional options. If he is not interested in violent weapons, he may sublimate his emotions into an involvement with a sport. Or, if he has that extra measure of clout, he may choose to use the same disruptive, confusing energy to start a war.

Because sex on the first date, or sooner if possible, is his goal does not mean that the man feels he owes the woman anything. In fact, if she succumbs too quickly, she might lose her chance at the movie. (Unless the movie involves some kind of martial arts, since he was definitely going to see it anyway.)

And it has nothing to do with whether or not he likes the woman. Because men do not apparently need any cumulative positive criteria to be drawn into the sex act. A musician I once met was explaining to me a complicated situation that had occurred with a groupie. I said to him, "Well, if you're going to have sex with people you know nothing about, isn't that going to inevitably lead to some trouble?" to which he replied, "Maybe. But when I'm eighty and looking back at my life, what am I going to say to myself? 'Gee, I didn't have sex with that girl because she was a sociopath'?"

He didn't indicate whether he would have drawn the line at psychopath, although I expect the answer is no, unless she was packing heat. Maybe not even then.

Which is not to say that women do not have sex with sociopaths. Sociopaths as a whole do very well in the dating game. With the notable exception of Unabomber Ted Kaczynski, you hardly hear of a serial killer who didn't have a full dance card. Okay, yes. Some, like Jeffrey Dahmer, felt that the company of headless torsos constituted an evening spent with friends. . . . But who hasn't been to a party like that on occasion? In fact, somewhere there are probably really embarrassed women who sat around boring their patient friends to tears obsessing on why it was that Ted Bundy never called them back.

Meanwhile, if a woman has sex on the first date it usually means she is very smitten with the guy and is under the wacky delusion that having sex will speed along a feeling of commitment between them. And it does. But only for *her*. Thanks to the fact that nature supplies women, but not men, with *fifty times the usual dose of oxytocin if they have an orgasm*. It has been proven over and over—and written about throughout literature and history—that sexual contact does not necessarily cause bonding in a man. In fact, even if everything goes fantastically well on a date, there is no guarantee that a man will want to ever see that woman again. For some men, there is a syndrome in which pleasant feelings of happiness and comfort trigger feelings of strangulation and terror. The better things go on the date, the quicker the guy must turn to run, an act that, of course, provides him with the same endorphins at a mere fraction of the cost.

But more frequently what he would like is to keep having sex with her on a nonexclusive basis while he waits to see if a big thunderbolt strikes him from out of the blue.

This is why the current wisdom is that it is not a good idea for women to have sex too soon. Instead, she should be cooling her heels and *listening really carefully*. Because for some reason, men feel compelled to announce their worst deficiencies on the first or second date. They will flat-out tell you *exactly* what kind of trouble you are in for. The problem is that women don't listen, or if they do, they don't *believe* them. There is no more perfect example than the guy I was seeing who said to me on the first date, "I have been running away from women for thirty years." And of course in my head I thought, "Oh, yes. Sure. Running from *women*. But you don't mean from *me*. Come to me, you poor sad-eyed drifter." But just the vibes produced by even having such *thoughts* in his presence caused him to begin training for a marathon.

The sheer quantity of dysfunctional people that one meets these days means that you may have to date a great many people. Which is why it is a very good idea to learn to be irresistible. But say you want to be more irresistible—what do you do? It's not like you can just sign up for a class that teaches a thing like that.

Unless you live in Los Angeles.

Chapter 4
How to Become Irresistible to the Opposite Sex

AS USUAL, THE TITLE PULLED ME IN. WOULD THAT I HAD READ THE whole course description of this seminar before I volunteered. "This innovative Seminar/Mixer is designed to teach you simple, proven techniques for attracting the opposite sex" is what I would have seen. *Seminar/Mixer*—words to put ice in my veins. "After the discussion period," it went on, "you'll mix with your fellow students in a relaxed social atmosphere, and you can try out what you've learned with adventurous people like yourself." The kind of adventurers so adrift in a sea of insecurity that they want to spend money on "irresistibility training." Not exactly Lewis or Clark.

The black guy with the dreadlocks who takes my money lets me know in no uncertain terms that I am entering seminar hell. "Thank you for coming," he says, smiling warmly. "You are very special to us." I am in even bigger trouble than I thought.

The aforementioned "relaxed social atmosphere" turns out to be about ten men and four women seated at the tiny desks of an empty third-grade classroom. Drawings and selected writings of the third graders are tacked up on bulletin boards. There are a big square teacher's desk and some graffiti-covered lockers. But from the moment I enter, I am primarily aware of just one thing: the very strong scent of B.O. Some of my fellow adventurers have been too busy to shower.

I take a desk in the very back of the room, hoping to remain unnoticed. Far away, I hope, from whichever of my fellow adventurers are supplying the room with its aroma.

But immediately I am asked to introduce myself. "I'm Christine," I say, happy to punish my faithless friend who announced that she was maxed out on seminars and refused to attend the class at the last minute. "Hi, Christine," both members of my husband-and-wife team of instructors chime brightly.

They are named Donny and Bonnie. Donny is wearing a beige turtleneck tucked into his gray pants, and the hair on his head is combed forward to cover his bald spot. For some reason he kind of reminds me of a forty-five-year-old Greek version of Gene Kelly. His wife, Bonnie, who appears to be a couple of years his senior, is blond and dressed in a white sweater and pink skirt. She is wearing white nylons and high-heeled pumps and when she speaks, it turns out she is British.

"Whether you believe it or not, you have always designed the quality of your relationships through your attitudes and belief systems," Donny opens. "Thoughts produce reality and attitude is everything. Let's say the A part of the mind says, 'The women I love always leave me,'" Donny continues, gesturing wildly with his left hand as he explains what turns out to be their central theory. "The B part of the mind will gather evidence to make sure this is true." Many people besides me in this class are writing stuff down. Especially the fortyish woman in the red suit, red heels, red glasses, and matching red nail polish.

A pale-skinned, light-haired guy in a white T-shirt—sort of a surfer-nerd—nods vehemently in reinforcement of everything Donny says. As in, "Yes. I completely agree. That is *absolutely true!*"

"An affirmation is a positive thought you immerse in your consciousness by repetition. How many people in this room use affirmations to some degree?"

"Yes, yes," white surfer-nerd nods, "absolutely yes." Donny holds up a cassette—one of several that are for sale here this evening. It is a tape of "all the highest-quality thoughts to attract the opposite sex," entitled "Heartfelt Celebration." I cannot wait to buy one later.

"What is a better thought than 'I can't have anything I want'?" Donny asks us with great animation. "On the count of three let's say it together. *I can have what I want!* Again! Please! I . . . *can* . . . have . . . *what* . . . I . . . *want.* Once more with feeling! *I can have what I want!!!*" Everyone in class is happy to chant along, with his every emphasis change. "If you did this before you went to a social event, you would be a little more irresistible right away," he tells us. "Let's try another one. *I like myself, and people like me.* Come on now, *once more* with a nice big smile on your face." He closes his eyes and waltzes a few steps, as though swept away on the tide of great emotion. "I like *myself* and *people like* me."

Seated in a chair, her hands folded in her lap, Bonnie watches him with great adoration. "*I am lovable and irresistible.* Again please. *I am* lovable and irresistible."

"Yes! Yes, you are!" shouts Bonnie supportively from the sidelines until she cannot contain herself anymore and jumps up and gives him a kiss. "You didn't say anything about no kissing."

Now Bonnie takes the floor. She was skeptical about affirmations at first, she tells us, but now she bombards herself with them. She pins them up on her cupboards, her refrigerator, her phone. As she speaks, Donny watches her with affectionate bemusement. They clearly find each other both lovable and irresistible.

Donny wants us to try a getting-to-know-you exercise. We are to get up and reach out our hand to each member of the class and complete the sentence, "Hi. I'm _____ and something that makes me irresistible is. . . ." Certainly a greeting I had hoped to live a full, long life without ever having to say out loud. But it's too late. Before I can head for the restroom, the games begin. Everyone is on their feet, and the most poorly socialized guy in the class is headed my way, his hand extended like a fishing lure. "Hi. I'm Larry," he says, "and something that makes me irresistible is my wacky, irrepressible sense of humor." He looks like the kind of guy who would corner you and tell you riddles. I know he must be a real laugh riot because all your funniest guys refer to themselves as "wacky and irrepressible."

"Hi, I'm Christine," I answer back, "and something that makes me irresistible is . . . my extreme hatred for stuff like this."

But before he can formulate a wacky and irrepressible rejoinder, I am shaking hands with Manuel. It is impressive that there are nerds here of every conceivable nationality and race. "Hi, I'm Manuel," he says, "and something that makes me irresistible is that I have a lot of weird fantasies." Certainly *my* definition of irresistible. Please, God, let me never have to know any further details. "Hi, I'm Christine," I reply, "and something that makes me irresistible is that I'm out of ways to finish this sentence."

"Oh, come on. You can do it!" a heavy woman in a two-piece denim suit tries to encourage me.

"Being attractive and irresistible comes from the *inside*," says Donny. "Change your self-esteem and you change your life." Although I cannot help but think that a little soap and water on the *outside* would go a long way to helping the irresistibility of a number of my fellow adventurers this evening. "We are advertising ourselves," says Donny, as we settle back into our seats. "Having high self-esteem is very attractive."

"You're a lot more handsome and gorgeous than you really think you are," says Bonnie to *everyone,* as she shares her *very favorite* affirmation with us: "I, _____, now unconditionally love and approve of myself in the presence of others."

"Thank you, Bonnie," says Donny. "Most people beat themselves up unmercifully."

White surfer-nerd nods agreement so hard I fear he may sever the disks in his neck and snap his head off. He is beginning to remind me of one of those spring-loaded dolls that I used to see on the dashboards of cars. "You want to *become* the love you are looking for," says Donny. Certainly a good way to cut down on dating expenses.

Wacky, irrepressible Larry has a question. "I find that when I'm least interested in a girl she is most responsive," he says. "And when I'm most interested, she's least responsive," he continues. "It's like, 'Screw you. Get lost'"—he is speaking much too fast and much too loud. It is immediately very clear why Larry is having problems. To say nothing of the fact that he has told us he is fifty-five years old. Even if he were not a hopeless nerd, maybe "girls" are no longer his best option. He has so many extremely obvious personality problems that affirmations designed to convince him he is just fine the way he is will be doing him no particular service.

"You have to give things time," Donny tells him. "You need to slow down. Let's all try this one. *I love and approve of myself in the presence of others.* Come on. I can't hear you. I *love* and approve of myself in the presence of *others*. I love and *approve* of *myself* in the presence of others."

"Let's talk a little bit about how to increase our magnetic appeal," offers Bonnie, grinning with bug-eyed enthusiasm. "What messages are we giving off to people? Are you approachable? Are you difficult to get to know? Look at my face."

She makes an intentionally glum face, as subtle as the Greek tragedy mask. Then suddenly brightens to a *Big Grin*!!! The comedy mask!! "A smile can do wonders! Smile! Say hello! Make eye contact! The eyes really are the windows to the soul."

"What if you have weak eye muscles?" asks wacky, irrepressible Larry. Bonnie looks at him quietly—apparently at a loss for words. "Touch is another thing," says Bonnie, moving right along. "Touch someone's shoulder. Reach out and touch their hand."

"I have a great deal of anxiety touching people—especially if they hug me," says wacky, irrepressible Larry.

"And remember your posture," says Bonnie, plowing ahead. "Posture makes a big impression." She demonstrates, going from terribly hunched over to miraculously straightened up. She is a virtual Goofus and Gallant.

"Okay, let's try another little exercise," says Donny, making my heart sink as he says the five words I least want to hear: "Pair off with another person." Rajiv, a fortysomething Indian gentleman in a plaid coat who is seated nearby, turns to me with the determined stare my dog Lewis uses when he is trying to browbeat me into serving a second dinner. He has the sort of hair that looks like a toupee even though I suspect it really is *his* hair.

We are asked to stare deeply into each other's eyes and repeat over and over the phrase, "I am an attractive and lovable person." Over and over and over. Every third time we say it we are to personalize it by adding our name, as in, "I, Rajiv, am an attractive and lovable man." And this is the signal for our partner to call out some support. For instance, "Yes! That's right! You really are!" or "You *are* an attractive and lovable man!! Yessir!!"

I am trapped again. All around me the exercise is in full swing.

And Rajiv has begun. "I am an attractive and lovable man," he says, staring deeply into my eyes. "I am an attractive and lovable man. I, Rajiv, am an attractive and lovable man."

"Tell me about it!" I pipe in. "You're the best."

Then it is my turn. I so much do not want to do this. I can barely get an entire sentence out. "I am an attractive and lovable . . . you know . . . whatever," I find myself muttering. "I *hate* this, I hate this, I hate this. I, Christine, am an attractive and lovable blah-blah-blah."

"Yes, you are!" Rajiv pipes up, staring deeply into my eyes. He does not speak enough English to know I am screwing around.

Donny beams at us with pride as we accomplish our goals. "Very good," he says. "But tell the truth, how many of you still heard that negative little voice in your head, undermining you, telling you that it's all just B.S."

Some hands go up.

"Not me," I think to myself. "No matter how silly this seems, at least I know my friend Rajiv would never lie to me."

"We're going to take a break in a couple of seconds," Donny tells us, much to my tremendous relief. "Although Bonnie and I are very entertaining speakers, we will have plenty of exercises and receiving processes coming up after the break that will help you become even more irresistible."

I don't know which thing terrifies me more—the idea of becoming even *more* irresistible, or finding out what new nightmare a "receiving process" will turn out to be. Maybe being too irresistible isn't even in a person's best interests.

All I know is I want so badly to go home that it sounds like an affirmation in my head. "I *love* myself, and I believe I should be able to *leave* this place *right now!*"

Although I feel in my heart that I should see the class through to its conclusion, I am drawn, like iron filings to a magnet, closer, ever closer to my car. I tell myself it's okay. I am just going to sit out there and listen to the affirmation tapes I have just purchased. And they are something to behold. On one, Bonnie, sounding for all the world like Glinda the Good Witch from *The Wizard of Oz,* gently and patiently sets up one or another premise that defines the acceptable limits of lowered expectations. For instance: "Be willing to praise yourself *simply for being alive!*" After she says it, then Donny, sounding like the man on everyone's voice mail, repeats the same affirmation two more times, as though they were a two-part thought and not two complete sentences. For instance: "I am willing to praise myself *simply for being alive?*" and then "I *am willing* to *praise* myself *simply for being alive!!!!*" Light orchestral selections play in the background.

Which is when I discover that the seminar *has* had a positive effect on me. Because in the last couple of hours I have learned to love myself so much that I now have no choice but to give myself permission to leave.

After all, if I deserve all this praise simply for being alive, I definitely deserve an engraved plaque and a cash award simply for going home.

As I am driving myself home, I begin thinking about how much work it takes to keep a social life going. It's truly exhausting. All the mental manipulation. All the wardrobe changes. All the driving.

And the female version of this dance is so much harder than the one required for the male. Because instead of simply seeking *fun,* women want to fall *in love.* Which is why what starts for everyone as a fun little scenic drive in the country often swerves suddenly into a nasty hit-and-run accident, if not a head-on collision.

Chapter 5
Why Can't a Woman Have Sex Like a Man?

IN CASE YOU NEVER NOTICED, WOMEN TAKE SEX JUST A TEENSY BIT more personally than do men.

But in my opinion the very nature of the physical act itself may be part of the reason. Think about it for a minute—the act of lying on your back, belly up, and agreeing to open your legs is a powerful statement of submission. That's what my dogs do when they abandon all hope in a fight. This decision to allow yourself to be so physically vulnerable in such a dramatic way—especially if it's with someone you may not even know all that well, let alone a sociopath—has a great deal of not-so-subtle emotional impact. It requires the woman to at least pretend she believes that anyone to whom she has given this kind of power is a pretty good person, or at least not someone who prefers the company of headless torsos. We need to feel safe, so we can enjoy ourselves. And *this* is the source of the whole damn problem.

Because no such complex series of feelings is required on the part of the man. He *enters* the woman. He doesn't feel vulnerable, or have to invent a bond to feel safe. In fact, he doesn't *want* to feel safe, since he can just get the hell out of there whenever he wants. For him it's like plunging into a hot bath. There's a strong, pleasurable physical reaction, but when he gets out and towels off, the bath almost immediately becomes a distant memory. He never really

35

thinks about the whole thing again until the next time it occurs to him that he might like another hot bath. And then it's just the idea of *any hot bath* more than it's a need to duplicate that last hot bath. Meanwhile, the woman *is* the bath. She is lying there, like a pool of water that is rapidly losing heat, gradually starting to feel abandoned, slowly draining, as she surveys the remnants of his sweat and hair floating in the wake that was left by his departure. (YOU: Oh, for God's sake, Merrill, can you be a little *more* melodramatic? ME: Cut me some slack, okay? The bath metaphor isn't working as well as I'd hoped.) But the *point* I was trying to make is that I think this critical difference in the way the physical act is experienced—the idea of letting someone *in* as opposed to getting *in* and getting *out*—is the *source* of all the eventual misunderstandings and messiness between men and women that is so often the end result of having sex. And here's the real kicker. *Men* definitely get the better version of the experience. Because their version syncs with the way they have the world set up. They get to play by a much more fun set of rules, as they skip happily from the scene of a casual sexual union unencumbered by the need to incorporate it into their lives. They don't even have to *like* the person all that well. Just like you would have a perfectly good hot bath in any old stupid bathtub. Okay, okay—I'll lose the bath thing. . . . How about this instead? It's like seeing a movie that wasn't that bad, like, say, *The Pelican Brief*—it held your attention, Denzel Washington was appealing—but afterwards you don't really remember what it was about and have no interest in seeing it again. It's over. You just open up the listings and see what else is playing. Imagine the liberation! No waiting for a phone call that may never come. And if it doesn't, no tedious follow-up discussions with girlfriends about whether it's okay for *you* to call *him*. No fretting and replaying the entire evening in your head, sentence by sentence, trying to figure out whether you said the wrong thing. No desperate last-ditch efforts to unravel what from your end appears to be his unfathomable behavior by visiting psychics and checking horoscopes. Imagine the luxury of being free of that, *and* getting to have fun sex too!

I started thinking about this because I was seeing someone who was commitment phobic, yet I really enjoyed the time we spent together. So I started thinking that if I could just relinquish all my female programming, I could continue having a good time. But nooo. Because I am a prisoner of female sexuality, without even wanting to, before I knew it I had bonded with the guy. Which is when it occurred to me that if I'd had a choice in the matter, I would have preferred to have the programming that allowed me to keep having fun, no questions asked. I would have liked the option of being a manizer. Then I could see a man who appealed to me physically and never for one second be concerned about having to relate to him on any other level. So what if he was a carnival worker who was missing a thumb or had a lengthy criminal record? Big deal. I wouldn't need to engage him long enough to ever find these things out. It would be so fantastic *not* to have to develop *feelings* for every damn guy you got the hots for. To no longer be driven to call the proceedings "a relationship." To *not* be burdened by the need to see it deepen—instead to be *happy* that, month after month, things continue to go nowhere! So what if the guy was stupid? You wouldn't need to talk to him. Just have sex with him, then get up, have a beer, and go out and work on the car. What a life. Just imagine . . .

MONDAY

Dear Diary: Won four hundred bucks on the Knicks game. I think the Rogain is finally starting to work—my hair looks thicker on top. That blond guy down the street I had sex with a couple of times started ragging on me because he says I haven't called him. I just *talked* to him three weeks ago for *twenty minutes!!* What a damn psycho. What do men *want* anyway??

TUESDAY

Dear Diary: Won two hundred bucks on the Raiders. B. called to rag on me. Apparently he heard I was out last night with R., which of course I was, but I *told* him I *wasn't* and he had the *nerve* to call me a *liar*. So I played indignant and hung up on him. How dare he? Leave it to me to find another crazy one. Men these days are *insane*.

WEDNESDAY

Dear Diary: That hot-looking waiter from last night came by for a minute. It's so great because his English is so bad I have no idea *what* he was saying. Fantastic! Who wants to talk to him? I just hope he doesn't go all psycho right away like whoever came by and let the air out of my tires. (Rob? Ed? Kevin? Mark? Pedro?) I guess it's probably time to change the phone number again. Played eight holes of golf. I'm making a lot of progress with my game.

So what can we learn from all this? Well, how about this?

If you are a woman, the next time you are overcome by the need to be a slave to an unappreciative cause that will barely acknowledge the energy you contribute, sign up to answer phones for a political candidate.

Meanwhile, proceeding with the theory that forewarned is forearmed, it seems like a good idea to develop your own arsenal of tricks to work with while you are waiting for true love to come knocking. Which is why I signed up for a class that seemed to be threatening to teach me a few things I wasn't sure that I knew yet.

Chapter 6
Man into Putty

THE COURSE DESCRIPTION IN THE CATALOG SAID "HOW TO TURN A man into Putty in Your Hands." Sounded pretty good, although I couldn't help but think to myself, "Gee, putty is *awfully* hard to get *off* your hands."

Nevertheless, I read a little further. "Do you wonder if you're really satisfying your lover?" it asked. "Do you have questions about oral sex you're too embarrassed to ask a friend?"

I've got the kind of friends it's pretty hard to be embarrassed around. Which is why I guess when I signed up I felt the need to bring one of them with me.

The course was being held at a newish hotel in Santa Monica. The man who took my credit card number over the phone told me there would be signs in the lobby to direct us to the class.

And, in fact, when we arrive, the lobby is awash in signs pointing to various functions. A conservatively dressed gathering of women turns out to be the Santa Monica Republican Women's Council. Behind them a sign points the way to the Indonesian Gospel Choir.

And just as we are starting to get kind of frustrated, I see it. A piece of paper with an arrow drawn on it and the handwritten words TURN A MAN INTO PUTTY. SECOND FLOOR. As we exit the second-floor elevator, many more handwritten signs lead us to a conference room with a closed door. MAN INTO PUTTY was what they say by the time we reach the sign-in table.

When we enter, the room is already full. There are about thirty women, all shapes and sizes, ranging in age from about twenty-five to fifty, seated around a large, oval conference table. They are mostly white, but there are several each of blacks, Asians, and Latinos. All are nicely groomed and casually dressed. Quite a few are wearing sport coats, although the woman sitting beside me had on a black patent-leather skirt, fishnet stockings, and heels.

The instructor, L. Lou Paget, a pretty fortyish former paper saleswoman, is standing at the head of the table beside a lectern, handing out a stapled course syllabus. She is dressed in a white T-shirt and brown slacks with a belt. Her light brown hair is pulled up into a clip so you can see her starburst earrings. She smiles at us latecomers as she sets many bottles of lubricants in the center of the table.

"Do you guys all know that this is a seminar about oral and manual sex?" she asks us. Actually, I didn't. So I quietly slip my putty knife into the back of my purse. She hands the last remaining syllabus to me for Christine and me to share. THE SOPHISTICATES' SEXUALITY SEMINAR it says. And inside a black and white border in the north, east, west, and south positions are the words "Dignity. Fun. Freedom. Access." Apparently the blow-job giver's credo.

The seminar, L. Lou tells us, began to take shape about ten years ago when she was having a cappuccino with a gay male friend and the subject of skill in the arena of oral sex surfaced. After she talked him into sharing his secrets with her, she realized that there were no good sources for this information. And so she began her fact-finding mission in earnest.

As she talks, she opens up a large cardboard box and removes "the DDJ—dildos du jour," each one sanitarily wrapped in clear plastic. "I should point out," she says, "that all of these dildos have only been used by hands or mouths." Then to further document her claim of cleanliness, she produces a Polaroid of all the dildos in the top rack of her dishwasher. "They're very politically correct," she tells us. "You have your choice. Six inches or eight inches. Black, white, or mulatto." And as she removes each one, she places it on a white china plate. Because, after all, this *is* the Sophisticates' Sexuality Seminar, and we sophisticates prefer a simple china pattern.

"Some of you may have to share," she says, looking once again at me and Christine as we receive the last plate of dildo: pink, eight inches, made of bendable latex, and obviously cast off a real person because it even has veins.

"I hope and pray that this is the last time you and I ever share something like this," I say to Christine. "This is the kind of thing that could make or break a friendship."

"They're amazingly lifelike," says the Asian woman in a red shirt and suspender pants seated across the table, as she pats hers on the head, causing it to bounce like a recently sprung diving board.

"All lubricants we will be using today are water based," says L. Lou, "because we're going to work with condoms, and oil-based lubricants, even lipstick, can damage latex."

I have learned something already. So we are instructed to put a dollop of a lubricant that heats up when we blow on it onto our hands. It feels kind of good, despite the voice in my head that is saying, "Heat in the genital area? Hmm. All the sensuous feeling of a urinary tract infection." But that is only one of the lubricant options available in the section of the course entitled "Your Hands: His World." This is an area in which our teacher has done extensive creative thinking. She has compiled an impressive list of the possible ways to make two hands on a penis simulate penetration. It reminds me a little of the knot-tying chart in the *Girl Scout Handbook:* All those different ways to tie a piece of rope, each with an individual name!

We begin with "Ode to Bryan," named after the friend who had shared the method with her. "It's a continuous motion," Lou tells us, as she demonstrates on her dildo, "hand over hand, over . . . up . . . and down with a twist . . . and then we start again."

All around me, women are working in earnest—attempting to master Ode to Bryan—comparing notes like any group of students doing a biology experiment. The room fills with the kind of cheerful bizarre chatter that you might find at a Tupperware party hosted by . . . oh . . . say Bob Guccione or Hieronymus Bosch.

"Don't forget the stepchildren," says our instructor, using her designated nickname for the testicles . . . a name she chose when someone pointed out to her that it is a part of the man that many women mistakenly ignore. "It's almost as if they treat them like stepchildren," was what her friend said to her. It is not a nickname with which I am comfortable. But then again, I get embarrassed having to say "a *short* cup of latte" at Starbucks.

Christine and I take turns attempting Ode to Bryan. "How do you do the return?" I ask her. "It's over the top, then down and twist," she corrects me. "It's a little like kneading bread."

"Keep as much contact with the head or glans as possible," our teacher reminds us, circulating through the class to check our form. "The most sensitive area of the man's penis is the first 1½ inches. That V-shaped section in the back." We all locate it on our dildos, kind of like in junior high school geography when we used to locate different continents on a globe of the world.

That accomplished, we move on to a new variation: the tantric cross. In this one our hands are at right angles to each other.

"How much pressure should you use?" asks a long-haired woman in wire-rimmed glasses and a flannel shirt. The teacher recommends keeping the pressure fairly light, but suggests getting the man "to show you how he likes it by putting his hand over your hands."

Now on to "basketweaving"—fingers woven together and pulsating intermittently. Each new approach is greeted with "oooh" or "aaaah" from the group. Like on QVC each time they bring out a new ring or bracelet during "The Discover Diamonique Hour."

Next "Temple and Mitzvah," a kind of "This is the church, this is the steeple" variation. "This is powerful stuff," L. Lou warns us. "I had one man pass out on me and another throw his back out—that was from a hand job–blow job combination."

"Something to look forward to," Christine points out. This section completed, we are now headed for "Your Mouth: His Universe"—quite a step up from the mere World that was Your Hands. But first we make a pit stop at one of the evening's more scenic vistas: The Italian Method, or how to put a condom on with your mouth.

It is semi-spectacular, beginning with the Japanese-tea-ceremony way in which the teacher applies the lubricant to the dildo from a fairly substantial height. Add to that the special moment when she shows us how to place a still coiled (but unlubricated) condom between our lips, reservoir tip in. Leading to a tableau vivant in which I am surrounded by a sea of women with condoms between their lips. It looks like Night of the Living Blow-Up Dolls.

And the next time I check the front of the room, our instructor is poised like a sword swallower, showing us how to glide our heads down, smoothly unfurling the condom as we go: a real crowd pleaser.

"If you can get it over the glans, it's fine," says the teacher. "You can just use your finger to get it the rest of the way down." Most of the class continues to try and perfect a way to do this without using their hands.

The ice is really broken now—the room is filled with a bizarre kind of oral sex banter. "I've been with a guy with *huge balls*," I hear a graying, stocky, fiftyish woman, who looks like she might be a regional head of the ACLU, say to the woman beside her as a heated discussion of "the stepchildren" gets under way, "and I have found that if you suck one into your mouth, the other one just comes in right behind it."

We still have much to learn. For instance—it turns out you can change the flavor of a man's semen by changing his diet. "Vegetarians taste better," "kiwi, pineapple, and celery make semen taste sweeter," "asparagus and garlic make it more bitter." All in all, as good a reason for menu planning as any.

Which brings us to the main course of the banquet, so to speak. "The tongue is never still," L. Lou tells us as she elaborates on "strumming the frenulum," an oral sex technique using the underside portion of the tongue. Then on to "rimming the glans." "When I do this, I am rarely nude," she says, sadly omitting the details of what she has determined is the appropriate outfit. I am imagining a gingham hoop skirt with ruffles.

There is so much more to this whole blow-job thing than the simple sucking action of yesteryear. For instance, "the snack bar approach," where a conveniently stashed beverage assortment allows you to change the temperature in your mouth from hot to cold and back if you like.

We learn that deep-throating is all a matter of angle. We learn about "humming," although we are not told what exactly to hum (probably *not* "The Eyes of Texas Are upon You." I become preoccupied trying to pick just the right song. Maybe "Girlfriend in a Coma," I think.)

Lost in this reverie, I also lose my place in class. "Where are we?" I ask Christine. "In back of the stepchildren," she tells me.

The hour is growing late. People are beginning to get up and put on their sport coats.

Soon the table is littered with abandoned plates still full of dildos like the end of a sloppy banquet at Jeffrey Dahmer's. I feel like I should ask for a doggy bag.

We have the option at this point of purchasing some of that heat-and-serve lubricant.

I buy a bottle of the Irish Cream—an impulse purchase inspired, I think, by the fact that I skipped dinner and now I am starving.

A bunch of us all ride down in the elevator together.

The cheery chatter slowly melts back into elevator silence, and by the time we all disembark in the parking lot, we are back to feeling slightly embarrassed. But we are also newly empowered. We are practically the sisterhood of the blow job. Maybe we are the equivalent of certified. An elite corps of specialists who can be called upon in emergencies, although I'd rather not imagine too clearly what those could conceivably be.

Yet even though we certainly covered a lot of ground this evening, as it turned out there still was a lot to learn.

Chapter 7
Secretz of Seduction

THE FLYER CAME IN THE MAIL. "HAVE YOU EVER MET THAT SPECIAL person and everything is going great and then, all of a sudden, he/ she stops returning your phone calls?" it asked. Well . . . um . . . now that you mention it, yes. "*Now* is the time to change the way your lover treats you. In this SIZZLING SEMINAR you'll learn how to become the seductive, wildly desirable person you've always dreamed of being."

Wowee. Not just desirable but *wildly desirable*. And as if I needed more enticement, *seductive* thrown in as a bonus. I've always wanted to be more seductive. The very word has such magical allure. It conjures images of a woman like Mata Hari—electric-eyed, lithe, draped in a diaphanous semi-transparent veil and harem pants, dancing witchily. Slack-jawed men stare at her, hypnotized by the sheer force of her sexual magnetism, even though she's really only a so-so dancer. The night air is full of gardenias and jasmine as she whirls by them, a wake of pastel scarves billowing behind her . . . and somehow there are snakes involved, too, but she doesn't scream or trip on them or get tangled up and have to make a bunch of lame jokes. Oh, no. She has no need to resort to sarcasm. She is a *seductress*. She has no reason to be ironically over-amped. She just keeps on whirling and peering, weaving a spell so intoxicating that when she wonders out loud who she can possibly get to walk her dogs for her, callous, brooding, cynical men fall all over themselves trying to be the first one to get to the leashes.

Which is why it came to pass that I signed up to attend "Secrets of Seduction." The instructor, Ava Cadell, had plenty of impressive credentials: such as a "certificate in sex education and clinical sexology (from where she did not say), as well as an "album . . . of passionate music and lyrics" called *The Soundz of Sex*. Talk about qualified. Only a bona fide seductress would even *think* of spelling *soundz* with a *z*.

It turns out I have my choice of attending the class at either a hotel meeting room or a hamburger restaurant. I decide on the hotel, because I am a vegetarian and feel that access to french fries would only hamper my blossoming seduction skills.

When my friend Christine and I arrive at the conference room in the mezzanine, the several rows of straight-backed chairs are filled equally with people of both sexes, mainly in their thirties and forties. I see blacks, whites, Asians, Latinos, Indians, and some men who appear to be Persians or Arabs. God Bless America. It is a virtual United Nations of seducer wannabes.

The instructor, Ava, comes to the front of the room dressed in a semi-transparent blouse, black high heels, and a skirt so tight that you could stack paperbacks in a row on the shelf that is her butt, although I can't think of what you would say to her to get her to agree to sit still for that. She has longish brown hair and speaks with a breathy voice that is equal parts Lady Di and Mr. Rogers.

She used to be an actress, she tells me later, but was cast mainly as the pretty girl in action-adventure films like *Fit to Kill*. Which was all fine and good, but as she began to get a bit older, she realized she was going to have to find a Plan B.

So here we all are at Plan B, and as I wait for the class to begin, I go up to survey the table laden with Ava's products-for-sale. There is quite an array. For instance, *Ava's Hot Lips,* a CD featuring "Six Sizzling Tales of LUST—The hottest sex stories ever told." The cover is emblazoned with a photo of a buxom Ava in red lingerie and black nylons making a face that must be meant to portray great passion because it involves far too much lip gloss for simple abdominal cramps. That she chose not to call it *Ava's Hot Lipz* is something I must take up with her later.

Meanwhile, I decide to purchase the class "workbook." The cover is a black-and-white drawing of a shirtless man smiling as he runs a comb through the hair of a woman whose facial contortion I now recognize as passion. Of course, it's hard to say what the appropriate expression should be under the circumstances, as I have yet to meet a man outside of a hair salon who exhibited even the teensiest bit of interest in combing my hair—something that I have always thought of as a *good* thing. Although perhaps I am missing something?

Inside the book, Ava adds an important credential to her résumé: "I think my greatest accomplishment was marrying a self-proclaimed playboy who had never been married," she says. I think perhaps what she *means* to say is "accomplizhment." The workbook and the class both begin with a list of "turnoffs" that Ava feels might hold the budding seducer back. Such as poor hygiene. "A messy car and home are a turnoff," she scolds. Uh oh. I'm in trouble already. "If your car looks like you live in it or your home is littered with laundry, it is a definite turnoff. . . ." "Any poor hygiene stories?" the workbook and Ava both ask, as I further embarrass myself by contemplating the various messy cars and laundry-strewn apartments belonging to guys who *should* have turned me off but didn't.

"Also, lack of sense of humor. This is something you either have or you don't," says Ava on the page and in the room. "If you don't, buy some joke books and go to some comedy clubs and see what makes you laugh. Then try out your new material on your friends." Another great idea. Nothing is more consistently seductive than seeing someone you barely know doing material they heard on *Evening at the Improv*. "Anyone have a story about a date without a sense of humor?" Ava asks. No one says anything, but I'm not sure anyone in this group, including the teacher, is in a position to judge.

Now we begin a discussion of the Art of Erotic Talk, always a staple of seduction. Say, perhaps, you'd like to strike up a conversation with that handsome stranger. Ava offers a scenario full of tips, using the always popular car wash setting. "What do you think of this car wash?" she suggests you might say for starters. "This is my first time here. I can't believe what a beautiful day it is, and I'm wearing this heavy jacket. How did you know it was going to be sunny? You know, you remind me of someone I met at Club Med two years ago. Have you ever been to Mexico?" Interesting, I think to myself, as I have never dreamed that tedious babbling could be used as a tool of seduction. Apparently I have been missing out.

Ava asks the class to share effective opening lines they have used. A blond woman in a Laura Ashley print dress claims "What is your favorite Bruce Lee movie?" has worked effectively. A flashy-looking girl in her twenties who later tells me she is a model-slash-dancer says she likes to go up to guys and say, "You are so fucking gorgeous." I look around the room. Two women seated at the end of my row are tucking into steak dinners they are balancing on trays on their laps. Next to them two Pakistani men in baseball caps are so expressionless I wonder if they understand English.

Which will not be a handicap for them in the next section, which turns out to be the very heart and soul of the class. "As little girls we played with Barbie dolls and maybe little boys played with trains," she tells us. "Well, now it's time to play with adult toys."

And she begins to hand out an assortment of very strange equipment to someone on the end of the first row, requesting that it be passed along, like we used to do with arrowheads and birds' nests in "Show and Tell." Except we are a long, long way from arrowheads here this evening. And because I am sitting on the floor in the front I have now entered a routine in which every few minutes a man in a navy blue suit who reminds me of Robert Shapiro (and does in fact turn out to be a lawyer) comes up to me and taps me on the shoulder. And when I turn around to see what he wants, I am continually alarmed and surprised when he shoves one after another vibrating decapitated body part facsimile at me.

"We'll begin with the pocket rocket," says Ava, taking out a hand-sized vibrator. "It's compact, nonthreatening, nonphallic."

"What does *phallic* mean?" asks one of my classmates, confirming my suspicion that no one had to submit SAT scores to get in this evening.

"It *doesn't* look like a penis," says the teacher. "You can use it in the car or when your lover doesn't satisfy you. Does anybody know how?"

The Bruce Lee fan in the Laura Ashley print dress raises her hand. "Turn on that little button on the side?" she volunteers tentatively. These seduction tips are even better than I had hoped for.

Moving right along, Ava takes out a lifelike dildo. "This is called the Hard Throb," she explains cheerily, "and what's nice about it is it's very realistic and great for double penetrations." And then tap-tap-tap on the shoulder and . . . slowly I turn—as Robert Shapiro is waving what could easily be a present from Lorena Bobbitt right in my very face. It is such a Three Stooges moment emotionally that I have to restrain myself from yelling out, "Nyaaa woop woop woop."

I look around the class. At the end of my row the two steak-dinner ladies are passing a small hand mirror between them, checking their teeth for bits of food. Things are otherwise in almost as big a lull as they would be if we were studying logarithms. This is made all the more amazing by the fact that so many people have a sex toy in their lap.

"Isn't this the prettiest vibrator you ever did see?" Ava asks the class enthusiastically, as she holds up an alabaster white, multidirectional penis facsimile that is so flashy it reminds me of Elvis during his Las Vegas period. It is the mirrored disco ball of vibrators. Set it in the middle of a room, and the kids could get up and dance to it. And then, seconds later . . . tap tap tap on the shoulder and there it is, inches from my eyes, already humming and vibrating for my convenience.

"Make it stop," Christine whines as I take it in my hands, holding it gingerly like it is a live cobra.

I am only beginning to comprehend its many and various functions when there is that tapping on my shoulder again . . . and this time when I turn to look up, I feel my face freeze into the expression I believe the young campers made in *Halloween I, II,* and *III* when they heard a noise in the bushes and then when they went to see what it was, they found Jason in a hockey mask, wielding a machete. Because Robert Shapiro is now insistent upon handing me a 3-D plastic vagina. "It was molded on the body of a porn star," Ava has just finished explaining to us, "and if you fill it with tap water, it squirts." Certainly an interesting alternative for some enterprising clown who is sick of the old seltzer bottle. All he needs to do is figure out where to attach the horn.

"I sent one of these to Howard Stern, and he talked about it on the radio," says Ava, "and that's how I found out that unless you use plenty of lubricant with it, you will bruise your penis."

The implications of this nightmarish new scenario are just beginning to dawn when there is that infernal tap tap tapping again. I don't want to turn around because Christine has rebelled and is refusing to take the toys from me. I am virtually knee-deep in plastic and rubber body parts.

"There's coffee and doughnuts right over there," Ava says, announcing a break as Robert Shapiro hands me yet another dildo; this one has a spikey dog collar of some kind. What a perfect time for snacks, I think, because nothing heats up the appetite for deep-fried dough quite like a plastic vagina—

Various members of the class get up from their seats to head for the doughnuts. Others head for the product table. Christine and I quickly decide on a third option: the bar in the lobby. We're both on diets, and neither one of us is crazy about the idea of chatting up strangers who are on line to buy vibrators.

After the break, class begins with a summary of a book the teacher is writing about the erotic uses for common household items. This is a premise she has worked on so diligently that she has even applied it to egg timers and pot holders. "Oven mitts are restrictive and clumsy, but that's what makes them fun" is one suggestion. "Both you and your lover can wear them while making love." "Mummify your lover with toilet paper" is another one. I don't know about the erotic potential of these ideas, but a sexed-up nude person headed toward you mummified in toilet paper, wearing only oven mitts sounds to me like an idea that would send Roger Corman scrambling for his checkbook. Maybe Ava is simply in the wrong business.

Of course, some of her ideas are more commonplace. For instance, "Make your lover a dessert, and you can eat it off each other" is a time-honored tradition for couples who just aren't getting enough hair in their food.

Which brings us to "erotic maneuvers that will put your lover at your beck and call," an exercise in which the girl-pal of the dancer-model is chosen as a volunteer, blindfolded, and instructed to seductively remove the clothes of a male blow-up doll. "He's oily, you guys!" she chirps as she handles him for the first time. The combination of his Beatle haircut and his perpetually opened mouth make him look distressingly like a recently deceased surfer boy, trapped for all eternity with the expression on his face that he used to make when he said the word *dude*. "Oh, you're very, very, very hard and very sexy," she says to him, as she takes off his pants . . . revealing a very, very nasty-looking, rubber blow-up penis. If there ever was an excellent reason to pray that Bozo the Clown never takes off his pants, this is it.

"See how much fun this is?" asks Ava. "Much more fun than just getting undressed and hopping into bed. Any questions?"

"How long does a lovemaking takes?" asks an Asian man in a gray corduroy jacket.

"The average is under five minutes" is the answer. FIVE MINUTES!!

Barely enough time to put on the oven mitts, let alone serve the dessert.

"Anyone else?" asked Ava.

The dancer-model raises her hand. "I know I'm pretty, and I'm funny, and I'm fun to be around," she says earnestly as the guy sitting beside her lightly massages her neck. "All my lovers say I'm a ten. But that I'd be an eleven if I only had big breasts. And it really really bothers me, and it really hurts my feelings." Her voice begins to quake a little.

I am shocked. Apparently, life isn't perfect, even for a beautiful hyphenate like herself.

"Well, try telling them, 'You would be an eleven if you had a ten-inch penis,'" suggests Ava.

"I have tried that," says the dancer-model remorsefully.

"Then try this," says Ava. "Say, 'Honey, when you're figuring out what to do for Christmas, I want you to buy me big breasts.'"

The dancer-model's face lights up. In a group psychic flash, each and every one in the class can simultaneously see her future.

In the final fleeting moments of class, Ava decides to read to us from the cards we filled out earlier on which we answered the question "What do *you* find erotic?" Most of the answers are pretty predictable: "Making love in the middle of the day." "Hot kisses." Until Ava comes to one that frankly has her puzzled. "A high IQ and a capacity for irrational mood swings?" she reads, shaking her head in confusion, "That's *erotic*?" She has, of course, just read the offering from Christine. I see her take my card ("Chain-smoking narcissists"), read it silently, and put it aside. I have fared even worse.

There's a parting piece of advice—one last secret of seduction from a woman in a position to know—"Men, please do call a woman the next day after sex. Even if you never want to see her again. Just say something like 'I really liked jumping your bones and I'll call you later.'" Good advice. Soften her up and *then* disappear. Now *that* is seductive.

As we file out of the class, I am treated to a view of two naked blow-up dolls lying in a pile between the lectern and the wall, looking like castoffs from a very cheap snuff movie.

"Okay, now go home and be creative," says Ava. Which is easy for her to say, but sadly, the damage is already done.

Now when I think of the word *seduction,* instead of the smell of jasmine and gardenias and the electricity of eye contact and mysterious manipulative behavior, I am going to have to think of Mata Hari leaping and billowing and whirling in her harem pants, her hands full of buzzing, rotating vibrators and squirting plastic vaginas.

Of course, strange as this all was, it did only represent seduction from a female point of view. A twisted female, perhaps. But a female nevertheless.

As I was now about to learn, twisted men have an entirely different way of looking at the subject.

Chapter 8
Speed Seduction:
The Cliff Notes

BECAUSE OF THE WAY MY NAME IS SPELLED, PEOPLE WHO HAVE SEEN my name in print (and have never met me in person and been overcome by my considerable charms) sometimes think I am a man. I would like to think that this is the explanation for how I came to receive a bulky xeroxed advertisement that began like this: "Dear Friend, What would it be worth to you if you knew you could get the hottest women completely lusting and eager for you within twenty minutes of meeting you, without even having to bother with a date?"

As a heterosexual female this did not describe a fantasy scenario in which I was hoping to participate. But as a hyper-ironic smartass, it was a piece of craziness that I could not easily dismiss. As I continued reading, I became increasingly eager to know what kind of manipulative techniques the author felt he had to share.

"Here's [sic] Some Of The Secrets You'll Learn In This Incredible Mind-Blowing Eye-Opening Complete Home Study Course," the flyer continued.

- How To Nail Her Within Minutes When You Aren't Close To Being Her Type!
- Messing With Her Sense of Time So It Seems Like She's Already Been In Love With You For Months When You've Only Know [sic] Her Just A Few Minutes!

- *Using Weasel Phrases To Get Into Her Mind (And Pants!) and TREMENDOUSLY TREMENDOUSLY MORE!!!*

So what could I do but *Get Out My Checkbook Right Away! I Couldn't Resist! I Had To Know What He Thought He'd Figured Out!* PLUS . . . *a chance to Learn Weasel Phrases!* I plain old couldn't wait to get my hands on *Ross Jeffries's Basic Speed Seduction Home Study Course, Consisting Of The Speed Seduction Book/Workbook, The Speed Seduction Weekend On Audio Tape Set,* and *The Speed Seduction Flash Cards* (Fee: $225. Plus Postage And Handling). (I also got, as a special bonus, two other self-published typo- and misspelling–laden books by Ross Jeffries entitled *How To Get The Women You Desire Into Bed* and *How To Get Girls Into Bed Without Trying.* What an offer!! Pinch me. I must be dreaming.)

Here was a chance to learn not only *Why Someone Would Want To Capitalize Every Word In A Sentence Like This* but also at least one version of the answer to the unanswerable question "What do men *think* they are doing when they do that weird stuff?" As well as its natural complement, "and what do they think *we* think is going on?" Usually the point at which such questions need answering is the point at which it is least possible to get anything remotely like an honest explanation from the perpetrator.

I'm referring to that point at which, when you ask your female friends, they are most likely to give you an answer like "I'll *tell* you what is going on. You found yourself another complete fucking lunatic. *That* is what is going on."

So the day my Speed Seduction course arrived I fairly danced with glee.

And now after having consumed and digested the combined oeuvre of Ross Jeffries I can say this: The old battle of the sexes has grown more convoluted, covert, and grisly than I ever imagined. The geniuses who brought us the mess in Bosnia and the problems in the Middle East owe a tip of the crazed-behavior hat to the goofballs who fork out $225 plus in the name of Speed Seduction.

"Love" is a process people do to themselves," says Mr. Jeffries, explaining his central premise. "It's not a 'thing' you trip over or a 'hole' you fall into."

"When you deal with women . . . ," he continues, "they expect you to play by the rules. But they feel perfectly free to do whatever *they* want. . . . For example, lots of women are more than happy to let you spend your money and time and generally lead you on letting you think you have a reward (sexual) coming. . . . Then when you make a pass, they freak out and scream about what animals men are. . . . Or maybe you find out that she was just using you as a social 'spare tire' because her boyfriend was out of town for a few weeks. Now any chick who pulls this off *deserves* to be on the receiving end of the most unfair tactics you can use."

And what *are* those tactics? "Any response that a woman makes to your moves can be turned on her and used to get what you want," says Ross Jeffries, "if you relax and DON'T ARGUE or ASK FOR EXPLANATIONS." "Never resist what a woman offers you. Listen between the lines and allow her to teach you how she wishes to be defeated."

For example, a suggestion (from *How To Get The Women You Desire Into Bed*) for dealing with a woman who says "I'm just not attracted to you" involves a creative use of guilt as a weapon. "One of the hardest things for anyone to do is watch a grown man cry," says the author. "After she rejects you, put your head in your hands and quietly start to sob." Talk about a turn-on!! *I'm Dissolving Into States Of Overwhelming Lust Just Reading About It!!!* Nothing gets a woman hot faster than a sobbing man—except perhaps a man with amoebic dysentery.

The bulk of the course is a clumsy kind of "power of suggestion" approach that supposedly helps the speed-seducer-wannabe sexualize an otherwise neutral occasion by *sneaking* in the subject of sex around women he presumes are not bright enough to see what he's doing.

This is called "embedding commands." For example, let's say a man *wants* to say, "I command you to feel very attracted to me." He can't just *say* it. It wouldn't really work for anyone except maybe an officer in a very unusual *Star Trek* subplot. So what he says instead is "You know, some people find as they listen to someone who is very fascinating that they can feel very attracted, Debbie."

ME: Well, yes, when they listen to someone *fascinating*. Just my luck that I'm here listening to *you*.

HIM: Fuck off. I was talking to Debbie.

Reading this stuff is alternately repellent and hypnotic, in the same vein as the "get the women to take their clothes off" sections of the Howard Stern show. It's a piece of pop anthropology, a version of locker-room talk, a chance to hear the darker side of male psychology run amok unrestrained by the need to be even a little politically correct.

When I was younger and stupider, it simply never registered with me how hard men might be working in the name of trying to score. So preoccupied was I by my own considerable insecurity that I always felt it would be jumping the gun to presume that a guy was still hanging around my house at four in the morning because he found me attractive. Maybe, I would think, he was still there because he . . . uh . . . was grateful to have found a room with central heating and was hoping for hot soup.

Guys have never had to scheme and lie to me to get me to play along because my position was always pretty clear. If I didn't like a guy, no amount of pseudo psychological ploys would have changed my opinion. And if there was chemistry, I would have such a head full of bees that the thunderous cacophony of buzzing would drown out even the foulest, most indigestible portions of his content. I was simply unwilling to let his real intentions distract me from the much more appealing fantasy scenario I had selected for him. Which brings us back to Ross Jeffries and his weird advice for poor sad men who have a couple hundred dollars to blow in the name of being both desperate and devious. Both traits are well represented in the delightful, classic chapter "How To Fake That You Are Warm And Friendly." "Just think of how you look and sound when you see a niece or nephew or a pet that delights you," he suggests. An excellent approach, particularly for the woman who enjoys being talked to as though she is a child!

Elsewhere are detailed instructions on how to give the impression that an emotional connection has been made. Because "for most women, creating a sense of incredible connection and bonding is a required step before you get to the sexual arousal stuff." "Guys are different," he explains. "Sometimes I think we just want to dump loads."

It's about at this point where the pure hatred of women at the core of the whole thing starts to be too transparent to be very funny.

"Oh the joy of battle, my brothers," says the author, in a chapter entitled "How to Handle Chicks Who Cancel Dates." "Flushing a chick down the toilet of humiliation is almost as great a kick as scoring!"

I decided to give the material to a couple of high-energy, young sexy guys to see how they would react. Mike, a thirtyish writer who used to work in a bank, found the material "totally preposterous." "The sexual innuendo that is always supposed to be taking place in his conversation—in any big city, the women would see right through that and think you're an idiot," he said.

Mike's roommate Larry, a handsome, charismatic personal trainer with a track record as an incredibly successful, self-styled speed seducer himself, also found the Ross Jeffries stuff stupid. But he has his own devious, foolproof seduction methods. "Like I'll look you in the eye while we're talking and I'll say, 'Stop doing that.'" "Stop doing what?" I say to him. "Stop looking at me like that," he says. "Looking at you like what?" I say, realizing I'm blushing a little. He grins at me. "*You* know exactly like what," he says. "You have sex on the brain." I feel embarrassed. Maybe I do. Here I *know* I'm participating in a demonstration. But suddenly I'm not really sure *what* is going on exactly. "The moment you say 'sex on the brain' they *do* have it on the brain," he explains to me, "and they think it was always there and I picked up on it somehow because it was showing." "Will you please stop thinking about sex," he says to me now. "I'm not," I say. "Yes, you are," he continues, "I can see it in your eyes." Now I have to remind myself *again* that this is only a demonstration. Even though the conversation was *my* idea!! And he has plenty more tricks where that came from. Tricks that worked so well for him (*before* he got married) that he once had seven different women ready and waiting for him in various stages of romantic blossoming—not unlike the way you grow a vegetable garden. Peas in the spring, broccoli in the fall, tomatoes all summer long.

"What I do is look them in the eyes and *really* talk to them," he tells me. "I make myself seem vulnerable. Women find that sexy. I try to seem non-threatening. Like I'll point out the best-looking guy in the room to her and say, 'That's who I see you with.' She's all flattered. Plus she thinks you're not interested, and it makes her want to win you over."

"What if someone picks up that you are manipulating her?" I ask him. "I'll say, 'You're right. Thank you for pointing that out to me. I have a tendency to do that. I'm sorry. Point that out to me if I do it again.'" "You *are* good at this," I tell him. He grins proudly.

So what have we learned exactly? Well, I guess it's this:

The brave new world that women have created where we have become self-assured enough to know and to also verbalize what we *need* has spawned an alternate universe—not unlike Superman's

Bizarro world—where men have learned to comprehend these needs and fake an approach to meeting them. One that they are willing to sustain until they get what *they* want. Which leaves the women and their needs pretty much right back where they started.

And what can be done to counteract this? Well, maybe if we change what we *say* we need so it *seems* like we *want* devious, shallow, promiscuous, manipulative guys, and then when *they* think that *we* think that . . . Oh, *I* don't know. No wonder I spend so much time hanging out with dogs.

Chapter 9
Dating Phase Two?

DATING PHASE TWO IS THE DOORWAY TO THE TERRIFYING STAGE known as the pseudo-love psycho ward. This is when otherwise reasonable, hard-working, theoretically independent women will begin obsessing about tiny behavioral details and snippets of conversation as indicators of whether this is a "relationship" or not.

In fact, she may initiate so much discussion about the "relationship" that she succeeds in destroying what little relationship there may be.

The best way for a man to know where he stands with a woman during this phase is to try introducing himself to her friends. If they do not groan and roll their eyes because they are so sick of hearing his name, things are not going nearly as well as he may have imagined.

How Do I Know If It's Love?

Some people just know because it feels so right, they say. I have met these people, and I have no choice but to take them at their word.

However, it is my experience that every day after the two-week mark that this feeling persists the chances that everything will work out happily ever after decrease by 75 percent until we reach the three-month mark, at which time the chance that the relationship will go forward is .000008937. Psychotherapist Pat Allen says that every relationship gets a three-month honeymoon period. That's if you're lucky.

It is after this point that a million terrifying questions begin to intrude. This is the phase in which women start to take love quizzes in women's magazines and hold marathon telephone bore-fests with a rapidly diminishing core group of patient friends. This is also the phase in which guys start magically disappearing.

The obsessive-compulsive nature of this phase causes some men and women to become paranoid and secretive and mysterious. This sets up a chain reaction. The more secretive and evasive and incomprehensible one person's behavior, the more the other one obsesses. If you go out for the afternoon and feel compelled to check your answering machine more than three times, you have entered this phase of dating.

This often brings the woman to the most expensive phase of the preliminary dating experience: the one where she starts asking psychics and astrologers and handwriting experts what they think is *really* going on. After many years of contemplating this, what I have learned about these situations is: Human beings are not all that complicated. If someone is behaving in ways that make it impossible for you to figure out *what is going on*—you do *not* need a psychic. The answer nine times out of ten is that there are other human beings involved that you do not know about—additional cast members—playing a wide variety of roles. If this were not the case, you *would* be able to figure out what is going on.

The only other possible explanation is if it turns out the object of your affections is a schizophrenic. And even then, it may be another person complicating things. It's just that the other person is them.

Obviously, things cannot go on like this for very long. Well, actually they can. They can go on like this for years. But it is incredibly annoying, and you really shouldn't let them. The next step is the painful one.

A Relationship or Not a Relationship?

Some people try to play both ends against the middle at first. As in "Well, it's a relationship, and yet it's not really a relationship." What they mean is if things are great and there is no set of conflicting circumstances for *me,* then it's a relationship. But if I meet someone else that I am kind of interested in and that person wants to know if I am in a relationship, then it's not *really* a relationship.

This is the phase of the dating process known as the pre-breakup negotiation. Someone will soon make a push come to a shove and the relationship will either go into a smoother gear or wind up being a very messy, out-of-control mudslide.

One possible exception to this rule is if the relationship is with a person who is under twenty-five. They, for the most part, don't really know what end is up yet and may allow things to stay just as they are. For a while.

When it comes to evaluating behavior in a relationship, men and women go through three distinct love stages. At least women do. I'm not so sure about men.

Age 15–28: The naive, good-natured love chumps. They will put up with almost anything and will often feel any problem is actually their fault. They love and believe in the idea of "potential."

Age 29–39: The serious, relationship-seeking love chumps. They have learned that putting up with really pernicious bad behavior goes on and on and leads to no good resolution and gets them nowhere and they are now interested in finding things that *work.*

Age 40–: The I-can't-take-any-more-crazies-please-don't-you-turn-out-to-be-crazy-too LOVE CHUMPS. They have been collecting data for twenty years, and they may decide that the relationship is hopeless based on what the guy orders for dinner.

This is one of the OTHER reasons that men over forty tend to like women under thirty. It is because a lot of men over thirty subscribe to the restroom washtowel approach to relationship growth. By which I mean they run the emotional curve like one of those continuous cloth towels that you pull on until you get a clean, dry section. And it works until you use the towel roll up and you're supposed to install a brand new towel loop. Which is the point at which, instead of starting on a new roll of towels, they want you to just dry your hands on the previously used dirty towels. Which is a long way of saying you make a circle and then start over again at the beginning and go around and around and around on the same tired loop.

And it is usually only the women under thirty who don't protest because they don't realize that the janitorial staff stopped coming in to change the towel roll in this particular restroom a long, long time ago.

The real truth is that lots and lots of people of both sexes over thirty begin to get really tired of having to meet new people, get to know them from scratch, and engage in the superficial rituals of dating.

But what do they do to find the theoretical soulmate who will lead them out of this muddy rut, they wonder. Luckily for the single people of Los Angeles, several seminars are available on this very subject.

Chapter 10
Finding Your Perfect Mate

"WHAT'S THE NAME OF THIS ONE?" CHRISTINE ASKED ME AS WE WERE driving over, eating our nonfat muffins in case we got trapped for long hours without any access to food.

"Prepare to FIND (and Marry!) Your PERFECT MATE in Six Months," I told her. "Gee—that's pretty soon," she said. "This is March. I don't know if I can pull everything together by September."

I thought about it as I drove. I wasn't too worried. September was wide open for me.

This one was being held at the Hyatt Hotel on Sunset Strip, nicknamed the Riot House in the seventies because it was the place where rock stars stayed. In the eighties it was famous again as the location where a frustrated comedian jumped off the roof to his death in the parking lot of the Comedy Store: a gesture of his hostility and disappointment with his career. And now in the nineties, here it is transformed into a place where you can learn to Find (and Marry!) Your Mate in Six Months. My goodness, what a growth curve.

As we arrive at the sign-in table, we see several people being turned away. But they are being turned away from something else. There are only three names signed up for Find (and Marry!), causing me to wonder if I would prefer to be in a room with a lot of people trying to get married by September . . . or just a few? Come to think of it, maybe the fewer, the better.

Inside the gray-yellow room at the end of the hall are about fifty upright chairs in three long rows, forty-seven of them empty.

On one side of the room, of course, is the table with teacher's books for sale. *Knight in Shining Armor* is one. *Liberated through Submission* is another.

We sit down. Slowly, a few more people trickle in. By the time the instructor makes an appearance, there are eleven of us. I am very discreet as I look around at my fellow classmates. After all, this is a room full of people who want to get married in six months. Not too surprisingly, there are three men and eight women, all of them brunette. Philomina Bunny enters and introduces herself. She is also brunette, dressed in a royal blue two-piece suit with a knee-length skirt and silver buttons. Immediately she orchestrates a re-grouping so we are all seated closer together. And would like us to get things rolling by going around the room, introducing ourselves and telling everyone what our "favorite pig-out dessert" is. How this dessert thing fits into the six-month plan, I do not know. Perhaps it is a mystical connection, kind of like a zodiac sign.

Ellen, a fiftyish, short-haired white woman with many folds of flesh above her lap like a jumbo stack of pancakes, says she likes fudge brownies. Danny, a thirtysomething white guy with brush-cut hair and an overeager expression, actually says, "Mom's apple pie." Christine likes birthday cake. And I do a strategic ducking-to-look-in-my-purse move that keeps me from being called on.

While all this is going on, a few more people show up: a Marcia Clark look-alike carrying a briefcase. And a very tall black guy in a long black trenchcoat who sits down right behind us. He has joined the group too late for a dessert revelation but from the amount of frantic fidgeting, he appears to be no stranger to sugar.

Philomina Bunny begins her talk. She has been married to her very own knight in shining armor for twenty-two years, and they have six children, so she knows whereof she speaks. She has also made many media appearances, including *Oprah* and *The 700 Club*. But during her years as a marriage counselor she noticed that in many cases her married friends were experiencing even greater loneliness than were her single friends. "When I was single, at least I *expected* to be lonely," they would say. She reads us some statistics: 37 percent of first marriages fail, 57 percent of second marriages, 80 percent of third marriages. "So, is there a spouse for everyone who wants one?" she asks, and then answers promptly, "The answer is a qualified yes." In her view, you need three things: 1) a strong desire for a spouse, 2) certain expectations that will dictate your attitude, and 3) belief in the power of prayer. "When you add God to the mix," she tells us, "you don't have to be looking over your shoulder all the time because *He* levels the playing field. He specializes in MIRACLES and allows you to cross the path of the person who is destined for you." To prove this point, she tells us the story of the time she and her husband went to New York City and mysteriously ran smack into two friends of theirs whom they had not seen in years.

This reminds me of the time I went to New York City and ran smack into a guy who unzipped his pants and then *glared* at me. And when I escaped into a restaurant, he stood at the window continuing to glare at me for about a half hour. What a coincidence! I haven't seen *him* in several years either.

There is erratic movement in my peripheral vision. The guy in the trenchcoat behind us has begun jiggling his leg with such velocity that the hair on my head is blowing as though I am in a shampoo commercial. He is literally causing the pages of my notebook to lift. I sort of lean back and turn a bit to see what he is up to, and out of the corner of my eye I notice he is briskly turning the pages of some kind of trade publication. He is *very* impatient. It is a little unsettling.

"Most single people already know their spouse," Bunny continues. "But our eyes are veiled from unrealistic expectations." I start thinking through the list of people I know. If one of them is my spouse, I am headed straight for a terrible divorce without even the benefit of a marriage.

"Who finds whom" is the next question Bunny wants to address. She begins by quoting a proverb: "A man who finds a wife finds a good thing and obtains favor from the Lord," which means to her that "the man does the looking, God does the fashioning and presenting. The woman just has to relax and believe that God will present her to the right man," she tells us. Well, this part I *like*! The idea of relaxing and doing nothing is just the kind of advice I was looking for.

"That guy behind us scares me," Christine whispers, prompted by continuous thumps on the back of her seat—the byproduct of his frequent leg crossings and recrossings. "Something about him makes me think maybe I should just wait for you outside until the class is finished," she says, only too happy to jump ship and leave me.

"Relax," I tell her, in jeopardy all by myself. "God has presented us to him. Maybe one of us will marry him in September."

I look back at him. He has paused on a page surveying condominium listings.

"When a woman accepts the fact that a man will find her, she stops being frustrated and develops a certain scent that only men can detect. Am I right, men?" Bunny asks. "Can you men sense this?" No one says anything. But let's face it—these men are only here because they are not sure *what* they sense.

"There's something about a woman who decides to trust God and let the men see her. Right, men? Am I right?"

Still no comment from the men. Although the guy behind us certainly has a variety of comments on *everything* else. Like when Bunny tells us, "There is someone out there for you. But you have to learn to compromise."

"Pppphhhhhh. Compromise," he mutters sarcastically. "That's cold." He begins to swing one leg over the other like a virtual human oil rig.

"Evaluating the people you date is the most important interview you will ever conduct," Bunny tells us. "Look at their track record," she advises. "*What you are looking for is a teachable spirit.* If they're a loner, they will not be open to counseling."

"Hmmmph. Good *luck,*" says the Oil Rig.

Bunny does not believe in sex before marriage because "it's like peeking at your Christmas presents before Christmas. It destroys the anticipation." I think back to Christmases past and all the gifts I had to return. I am not so sure this analogy works. But Bunny moves on . . . : "One of the worst spouses you can get is someone who has a lot of sexual experience," she says. "They will assume that they know how to satisfy you. If there are no two fingerprints alike, why would you think there would be any two bodies alike?" she says, throwing the whole notion of the Sophisticates' seminar right into the dumpster.

"Our bodies are like a combination lock, and the only way your spouse is going to get the combination is if you give it to him. That's how God safeguards against adultery," she tells us. Which may explain why adultery is so common. These are painfully inadequate safeguards.

Meanwhile, the message Bunny means to give us is that the best use of our time alone as singles is to look at it as the down time we need to get ourselves together—emotionally, financially, and spiritually. We need "to allow the clocks to be cleaned off the fireplaces of our hearts," for one thing. We have to rid ourselves of negative emotions. "Betrayal has a baby, and that baby's name is bitterness," she says. Certainly one of the worst baby names since Chastity.

"Are there people you cannot forgive?" she asks.

"*Yep!!!*" says Mr. Trenchcoat. "Boy, that's the truth."

"If I were to spend one day inside of your mind right now, would I have a good day?" Bunny asks. "What would I find there?"

"Chaos. Madness," Trenchcoat mutters behind us.

Now Christine is really getting nervous. She is concerned that Trenchcoat may be armed and if Bunny gets him too riled, we will not be around in six months to attend our own weddings.

A scholarly-looking black gentleman dressed in a navy blue suit who is seated in the front of the room has a question that concerns him.

"I was seeking a more specific plan of action for myself," he tells her. "During the six months of reconstruction, what should be your social posture?"

"You don't need to *do anything*," says Bunny. "Just put it in God's hands. Your goal is to become fulfilled as a single person," she tells him.

"Okay," I say to her, "but let's say that you do that . . . that you go ahead and put it in God's hands. And then week after week, and month after month goes by, and you meet no one. Then what do you do?"

"Ask God why this is happening," Bunny suggests. "He talks. He will tell you. He will give you an answer. Maybe he has other plans for you."

Trenchcoat exhales a giant snort like a racehorse. The class is coming to an end. Various students get up and cluster around Bunny, perhaps hoping to get more specifics about God's Dating Service.

Danny, the white guy with the brush-cut hair, comes up and taps me on the shoulder. He recognizes me from somewhere and tells me he likes my work. This makes me very nervous. He is not remotely my type, but has God presented me to him and now we must marry?

Danny begins telling me how he knows someone who knows Phil Hartman, and how he has a cousin who dated someone from Poco. I cannot really focus on what he is saying because my peripheral hearing is picking up Mr. Trenchcoat. He is talking to Bunny, using the word "prison" repeatedly, followed by the phrases "somebody got killed" and "someone is gonna get hurt."

And so, even though my Knight in Shining Armor is now hitting on me about how to write comedy, I finally believe Christine had the right idea all along. It's TIME TO LEAVE.

After all, September will be here any second. We have a lot of shopping to do. Out in the hall, as I wait while Christine uses the phone, I see Mr. Trenchcoat approaching.

And as I stand there, he walks up to me, looks at me, and shakes his head. Then he lets out a little hoot of laughter.

"Six months, huh?" he cackles. "What are you gonna do in six months?"

"I don't know how this happened," I tell him, "but I think I'm fully booked."

How to Meet, Date, and Marry

About a week later, at another hotel on the other side of town, eight people are seated on folding chairs in the same room where we learned to turn men into putty. Two fortysomething MFCCs (masters in family counseling) are going to teach us how to meet, date, and marry. They are a blondish man named Jack and a dark-haired woman named Eleanor. He is dressed in gray pants and a black shirt; she has a sporty brocaded vest, and her hair is pulled back in a hairbow. But what really distinguishes them so far is that apparently these two have not yet figured out how to merchandise what they do. They have nothing for sale on a table.

"If you want a relationship, you can have one" is what the ad for the class boasted. "Let this class give you the tools to make these decisions and more."

"I just hope they don't call on us," my friend Margy is muttering from the moment we take our seats in the very back of the room. "They better not call on us. If they call on me, I'm going to freak." I am now a seasoned pathetic seminar veteran, so I am not similarly concerned. But what does concern me is our topic: "How to Meet, Date, *and* Marry." They've bitten off quite a chunk. Time she is a wasting. They'd better get started right away.

This is before I notice something about our group that I find even more distressing. The woman seated in front of me is someone I recognize. She is the basset-hound–faced employee of my local dry cleaner's whose existence I have been contemplating with morbid empathy for the past five years. She has the kind of looks and demeanor that probably made her appear to be about fifty even when she was a teenager. I have seen her at the park jogging, and at the market shopping, her face always locked in a mournful yet expressionless mask. I have seen her at the swimming pool—looking all wrong in a very colorful swimsuit. I have often wondered about her life and hoped it was okay.

And now here she is—hoping to learn how to Meet, Date, and Marry in just three hours. These teachers had better work *fast*.

Which is why it's surprising that Jack seems to be in no real hurry. He first wants to tell us a lot of things about himself: that he used to be fat, and then he went into a twelve-step program, which is how it happened that he also teaches an eating-disorder class and one about John Bradshaw, for which he is pleased to say he has received quite a few unsolicited compliments. He *is* in a relationship now, but there was a time when he was tearing his hair out, attending singles dances and sporting such a resentful attitude that it turned into a good M.O., because he met other people who had resentful attitudes.

"The goal of this class," Eleanor tells us, "is to come away with one or two new approaches to things that you can do differently." I guess voluntarily attending a singles event in the hopes of meeting other resentful people is kind of a new one. But fifteen minutes have passed. Now we have only two hours and forty-five minutes to learn how to meet, date, and marry!

Ah! Okay—here we go. The instructors close the doors. Margy's worst fears are going to be realized. We are each going to have to tell the class why we are here this evening. We begin with Phil, a heavy guy in the front row, who is forty-seven years old, has never been married, and finds relationships painful.

Belinda, a perky welfare mother in her fifties, resplendent in a plaid shirt and matching pink earrings, tells us that she is worried that she might not have the social skills she needs to get back into the swing of things.

Robert, thirty-six, hasn't had a relationship for the past three years, since a woman he refused to marry left him. Scott, forty-six, is having trouble finding someone young enough to have a family with him who doesn't already have a family of her own. The lady from my dry cleaner (who I am horrified to discover is only forty-three) has had problems with depression and intimacy her whole life and now finds herself lying awake at night terrified of growing old alone.

I make a mental note to try to find another dry cleaner.

And now we are to Margy, who tells them she is too uncomfortable to speak to the group about her personal life. The shrinks congratulate her on having the guts to stand by her boundaries.

I say I came out of curiosity, so I don't get congratulated, because I didn't feel like admitting to any pain.

However, the shrinks do congratulate *everyone* on having the guts to attend. It's a right first step, they say. But now we are AN HOUR AND A HALF INTO THE CLASS and we haven't even scratched the "Meet" section yet.

But wait—here comes something! Two pages of printed material—the first one called "Where and How Singles Meet," a list of amazing suggestions such as "Singles events" and "Professional organizations. Schools. Libraries. Stores. Restaurants." There must be dozens of illegal aliens who haven't been in this country long enough to have written this list themselves.

"Recreational activities!" I say to Margy. "Who would have imagined you could meet people that way?"

Under a subheading entitled "Processes by Which Singles Meet" are such additional breakthrough ideas as "Introductions," "Matchmakers," and "While out with friends."

I raise my hand. "So what you're saying here is that someone can introduce you to someone else?" I ask. "That's exactly right," says Jack, who follows up with a story about how he once ran a personal ad in the paper, but although he got a lot of responses, he ended up throwing them out. Of all the people attending the class this evening, Jack is shaping up as the one with the biggest problems.

"Any other reactions to these suggestions?" he asks. Belinda raises her hand. She says she feels uncomfortable starting up a conversation with strangers. She worries that other people will find her boring.

The two shrinks eye each other knowingly. Here is their chance to showcase their one distinct contribution to the love seminar genre: the psychology team improv, using kind of a Nichols and May format without all the cumbersome punch lines. They set it up pretty much the same way a standard improv group does—by asking the audience to suggest characters and situations. But instead of "two guys from New Jersey running the first 7-11 on the Moon," they are going to do "two people who have just met and have to work out a number of pesky personality dysfunctions." Including Belinda's fear that she may be boring.

"Okay," says Jack, "we're at a monthly movie group and it is intermission. Eleanor is someone who really is into editing, and I have no interest in the topic."

And it goes something like this.

ELEANOR: So what did you think of the film?
JACK: It was okay. I didn't quite get it.

ELEANOR: I *loved* the editing. That long sequence of short scenes in the middle reminded me of a bunch of other movies I really admire—the pacing, the timing . . . it was excellent.

J: This is *so embarrassing*. I don't even *know* what editing *is*.

E: Well, why don't we get together for coffee later. Once I explain it to you, you will be surprised how important good editing is to a film.

J: You know, you seem fascinating and I'd love to talk more, but I'd rather talk about something we both know about.

E: I'm so glad you were able to tell me.

J: It feels nice to be heard.

E: Tell you what, after the movie *you* get to start the conversation.

"See how that went?" Jack says, apparently pleased with the egomaniacal bully he has shown himself to be. "Rather than be a boor, I was able to get her to agree to change the topic."

Except not only does this scenario not really apply to what Belinda asked, it is hard to imagine anyone actually having this conversation unless they were trying out a foreign-language sample from a Berlitz book.

But worse still—it is eight-thirty. There is only ONE HOUR LEFT for us to cover *all* of How to *Date and Marry*. If this had been a class on the History of Western Civilization, right about now we would be facing the likelihood of having to skip everything from the Middle Ages to the Industrial Revolution.

I am angry. Damn it! They owe it to my lonely dry cleaner to pick up the pace. As it turns out, Margy and I are both so close to depression that when a break is announced, we head to the bar at the end of the hall. I may have to give up love seminars before this pattern of drinking to get through the second half becomes dangerous.

Interestingly enough, just several feet away the hotel bar scene turns out to be lively and interesting. Members of a rock and roll band have just arrived and are ordering beers. I suspect there is more specific information here—at least regarding how to Meet and Date—than can be found spending another hour with those two annoying shrinks.

Which is when it dawns on the two of us that we have no intention of returning to that classroom. It's not even voluntary. We cannot make our bodies go back there.

On our way out of the hotel, we pass by the poor sad lady from my dry cleaner. Like Eleanor Rigby, she is wordlessly heading back into her cave after a brief but unsuccessful attempt to cause her life to change instantaneously. Maybe she will begin to spend more time in restaurants, stores, and museums. Maybe it will work for her. I hope so.

Meanwhile, judging by the level of advice we received, I feel I can fill in the blanks for what *would* have been covered after the break as follows:

How to date:

1. Find someone who will agree to meet you at a prearranged location. If you like them, try to hold a conversation with them for a number of hours. Places to go on a date: Movies, restaurants, your house, their house, places where there is entertainment.

How to marry:

1. Get a person you are in love with to make a lifetime commitment to you by agreeing to participate in a mutually agreed upon ritual in front of friends and family. Food should be served.
2. File appropriate legal papers so the government will know this has taken place.

Meanwhile, as your search for the perfect mate continues, you must keep your eyes and ears open. The road ahead may be not just bumpy but under construction and in need of repairs.

It takes a lot of time and effort to reroute the impulses that cause repetition compulsion. It doesn't happen overnight. So you may find that you have several rounds of love with completely crazy people still ahead of you before the high cost of therapy and your boredom with your own craziness finally forces you to knock it off for the last time. ·

This is why it's a good idea to learn an approach to navigate this kind of terrain before you go off-road for another drive.

Chapter 11
Tips on Dating a Crazy Person

CRAZY PEOPLE CAN BE VERY ATTRACTIVE. NATURE, IN HER INFINITE wisdom, helped a lot of crazy people adjust to our world better by giving them extra talent, charisma, good looks, or all of the above. And there are many, many, many crazy people to choose from, because, of course, they are always on their way out of a relationship. You may find that it is easier to have immediate chemistry with a crazy person, because crazy people are basically a chemical experiment raging out of control.

If you are uncertain, there are several good ways to tell for sure whether you do in fact have yourself a crazy person. One is to ask them why their last relationship came apart. "I don't even know," will be a typical response. "She [or he] said I was crazy." If you follow this up by asking if it is true, they will say, "Yeah, right. I guess I'm crazy" in a way that sounds both ironic and romantic. They are implying that they are the lone sane person in a crazy world. "Isn't that what they say about all geniuses and creative people?" you will say to yourself as a way to disguise the fact that you have just learned the dangerous truth.

If you still decide to go forward, the following tips will be invaluable:

Tip #1: *Become Attached Very Quickly*. If possible, decide that you are hopelessly in love by the end of the first date. This is usu-

83

ally how repetition compulsion works anyway. Something about this particular person will speak to you in the deep recesses of your soul. That this turns out to be the annoying voice of your mother performing a ventriloquist act that would give any Clive Barker plot a run for its money would be too distressing to realize. But don't worry. It will never occur to you in a million years. All you know is that even though you have just met this person, you want to be with him (or her) *always*. So go ahead and make a pact with yourself that you will do anything possible to make this relationship work. Anything.

Congratulations! Now you have mounted a spirited steed that you can ride all the way into hell. Bon voyage!

Tip #2: *Be Flexible!* This will become your mantra now that you have decided that your number one priority is to make your special crazy person happy. He or she is, after all, so alone. So very alone.

At least this has been the profile for the bulk of my crazy people, who have tended toward the wounded, brooding, loner category, a romantic ideal that attracted me when I was twelve and that I decided to hang on to, despite the fact that I didn't carry even one other idea I had when I was twelve forward into adulthood.

Nevertheless, that was the year I began to like the idea of the romantic delinquent, staring out the window into the middle distance at the fog, the mist, the snow, the rain—whatever seasonal precipitant might be available, exhaling mouthfuls of mournful smoke as he drags on one more cigarette. If only he could find the one woman who would really understand. Only in the last few years did I ask myself "Understand what?" and the answer came back, "Understand *this:* In all the years you hang out with me you will never, ever hear me use the word *you*. It's always going to be *me!me!me!*"

Which is a useful thing to remember as you begin to relate to your crazy person. Don't be too demanding. This will become easier when you finally realize that there is nothing you need to ask for from this person. You are having this relationship by yourself.

But the good news is that you will have less and less trouble doing this because you will slowly but surely lose all sense of yourself as a separate sane person. You will cease to remember what it was you were going to ask for anyway. You will cease to be burdened by your bothersome instincts as you continue to put them aside in the interest of trying to make your special crazy person happy. The only slight down side to all of this is that there is no way to make a crazy person happy. But . . .

Tip #3: *Never Give Up. Never Stop Trying!* Yes, yes, every book you read and every mental health professional you talk to will tell you that you cannot change another person. You only change yourself. Which is why this is the point where some women will begin to bend themselves into very strange, bacteria-shaped configurations trying to accommodate the desires of their special crazy person until they eventually reach the point where "Look, I just don't like you" sounds like constructive criticism.

Tip #4: *Forget about Therapy.* It doesn't help you fix your relationship with your crazy person. Most crazy people fall into one of two camps with regard to therapy. They either don't believe in it because as far as they are concerned there is nothing wrong with them (it is the details of the outside world that are all wrong!). Or they are seeing a shrink five days a week and have been for quite a few years.

Oddly enough, the net result of both approaches is the same. Except that one of them gives you a crazy person with a lot more money and free time.

On the bright side, if you are with a crazy person who subscribes to the second method, you will be able to put a lot of time and energy into waiting around hoping for change. And this can constitute a hobby of sorts, not unlike Ping-Pong or golf. Which is why you need to . . .

Tip #5: *Be Patient.* Waiting around for an adult human to reassemble the parts of a personality that took twenty-five, thirty-five, or forty-five years to put together can be a very slow process. Most likely you will not see the results of it in your lifetime. As a parallel model, ask yourself how long it would take you to talk yourself into going out and getting a radically different haircut. What would be your mobilization timetable? Now remember you are not just talking about the hair portion of the head; you're talking about the whole damn head! But maybe it is just as well, because if you do talk your crazy person into *anything,* and they don't like it *immediately,* they will hold it against you *for the rest of your natural life.* And if you believe in past lives, you will find they hold it against you there, too.

Tip #6: *Be Imaginative.* You will need a good imagination to help you twist every single thing in the universe all around so that it doesn't upset your crazy person. This requires a lot of second guessing. The crazy person may require you to know what he or she wants before they know it themselves.

The good news is that if you learn to get good at this, you will soon lose track of what the real situation is to begin with. You will have no idea what you actually think or feel. You will just proceed trying to placate the angst of your beloved. For example:

HER: Where do you want to go for dinner?

CRAZY PERSON: I don't care. Surprise me.

HER: (Thinks to self, If I say Mexican food, he'll say no because he always says no to the first thing I mention, but if I say Japanese food, he'll get mad because he'll think I don't remember that the last time we ate Japanese food he thought he had food poisoning, which actually turned out to be stomach flu, but I'm sure he still holds the food responsible, so I could say German food, except he'll get annoyed and say it's too full of fat so . . . so . . . okay . . .) CHINESE FOOD.

CRAZY PERSON: Chinese food? That's your idea of a surprise? We always eat Chinese food. I said *surprise* me!!

Remember, there is no winning with a crazy person, but just as important is this: If you don't *lose big,* it *is* a win! So hang in there!

Tip #7: *Learn to Roll with the Punches.* You may encounter some problems with meddlesome friends who will eventually tire of hearing your confusing, whiny relationship stories and feel compelled to tell you that they think *you* are the crazy one to continue in a relationship like this. There is a simple solution to this: Get new friends. And it doesn't matter whom you pick, because you will rarely see them anyway. A good crazy person requires a lot of time and obsession and will probably want nothing to do with your friends no matter *who* they are. You may have to sacrifice most of your friendships as an act of loyalty, anyway.

In summation, the important underlying fact to hold on to— the thing that will bind the relationship and hold it together—is that the two of you have one important thing in common. You are both in love with him/her and want nothing more than for him/her to be happy. At least you have a big common goal, right?

And plenty of choice when it comes to greeting card selection (see the Hallmark poets, pp. 7–9).

Chapter 12
Warped Perspective: Love and Sex on the Astral Plane

ONE OF THE GREAT CONTINUING HUMILIATIONS OF THE PURSUIT OF love is the blind date. It provides you with the opportunity to see who people you believed were your *friends* think would be a reasonable person for you to be with. This can be not just shocking and eye opening but deeply, deeply depressing as you find yourself cheerily matched up with the kind of person that the friend who made the match would never sit near in a crowded cafeteria, even by accident.

Much of the pursuit of love can be depressing, defeating, and demoralizing. That is why it is important to remember that Perspective is *everything*.

An excellent example of the use of perspective as a way to totally rewrite reality is demonstrated by the metaphysicians. Take *The Art of Sexual Magic* by Margo Arnaud. Please. In it she describes what could be viewed as a suspicious clandestine meeting as follows:

"Once I had the good fortune to work intensely for several years with a tantric teacher in sexual magic. He would visit me unexpectedly in the secret hours of the night and would invite me to engage in intense breathing exercises that would quickly generate a fiery energy in my body." One woman's metaphysical energy-exchanging experience is another woman's pathetic middle-of-the-night affair with a married man. It's all in how you look at it. Talk about seeing the glass half empty or half full.

But special praise must be reserved for *The Book of Astral Love* by D. J. Conway, the best example ever of a glorified perspective applied to potentially pathetic reality. I came upon it via advertisement in the back of a weird catalog. "If you are single and without a reliable partner, astral sex can be a safe rewarding alternative to a physical relationship," the ad said, claiming it would tell you how to have sex with "advanced beings who will become your teachers, friends, and lovers through the practice of astral sex magic."

And it's not just for single people either. "Suppose you have a mate or are married," the book suggests. "You want a little spice in your life and aren't the kind of person who believes in cheating on your mate. An astral lover can lend emotional and spiritual support, satisfy your emotional needs, and perhaps influence the physical situation so it turns out for the better." After all, "having an astral lover is not cheating or sinful," the author tells us. "You never need feel alone and despondent again. Your own special astral lover is only a thought away." For that matter, so is your own special country where ice cream has no calories and dogs can get driver's licenses! But that's a different story. Talk about a creative, uplifting reconfiguration of sitting at home alone masturbating. This is the most fully realized imaginary companion since *Harvey,* the play about the man who lives with a six-foot rabbit. *AND this* book gives instructions so the reader can play along.

First you are told to imagine setting up a lovely trysting place, which you will want to decorate in a "cozy" fashion. Now you simply inhabit your newly decorated residence and "when you are ready spiritually the astral lover will appear."

Which does not mean that you should be willing to take just anyone who shows up. "Think carefully before you establish a relationship with a deceased person," the author is wise to caution us. *"You do not want a succubus or an incubus."*

This is a generality with which I would have to take exception. Maybe they would be *different* with *you.* But just in case you are unsure of whether or not you have truly made contact, the author also explains that "sometimes the presence of astral beings is experienced as the sensation of cobwebs brushing around your face." Which doesn't sound familiar to me. If it can be expanded to include the sensation of fleas around your ankles, however, I am an astral slut.

In summing up, the book advises that you not "talk to others about your astral love life. This can expose your astral lover to hate and ridicule." And oddly enough, it may expose *you* to just the teensiest bit of ridicule yourself.

But nevertheless, I thought I'd give it a try.

My Astral Date

I sit quietly, filled with healing white light, and soon I find myself lounging comfortably in my cozily decorated astral-plane chateau. It is done in kind of a nouveau southwest antique country pine with just a hint of airport terminal. Judging by my cookware selection, apparently the Pottery Barn has a branch on the astral plane.

And there's more good news. Either I have a cleaning service up here or the dogs have not visited yet. The place seems to be delightfully free of dog-hair wads.

I light a few of those really big, overpriced, aromatherapy candles (and judging by how many of them I have, there must have been some sort of a sale) . . . and as I listen quietly to the peaceful tinkling of wind chimes, a gentle breeze blows through my flowing robes. Apparently, I have made a rather risky wardrobe choice for a first date. I have never worn flowing robes *out* anywhere before. I am concerned that they make me look fat.

But then again, I don't even know if there is going to be a real date. Is astral boy actually going to show up? I don't want to get all overdressed and then feel like a damn fool waiting for a figment of my imagination.

So I release myself from petty anxieties and enjoy the way the warm air feels on my golden hair (what the hell—I went with honey blond here on the astral plane).

I enjoy the intoxicating smell of jasmine and gardenia. . . . And then . . . I realize I am not alone. There is a presence. *He* is here. He didn't knock or anything. But he does not frighten me. He is muscular, tall, and incredibly sexy looking. He has a kind smile, intelligent eyes, and an athletic look, but I can tell he is not obsessed with televised astral sports (which pleases me since they are even more annoying than earthly ones. They have to do with batting a ball around with your brain waves). Slowly, I turn to him. As I speak, we look deep into each other's eyes.

ME: Hi.

HIM: Hi.

ME: And you are . . . ?

HIM: Your astral lover, Thor.

ME: Nice to meet you. Is that your real name? *Thor*?

HIM: Well, yes. I just said it was.

ME: I just thought maybe it was a pseudonym. Like a rapper or a deejay.

HIM: No, it's my name.

ME: Well, great!!! Nice name!

(*Uncomfortable silence.*)

ME: Um . . . can I get you something? Do you guys drink?

HIM: Sure. But I'm in the program . . .

ME: You know, something about you is beginning to seem familiar to me.

HIM: Well, duh. That's because we have been lovers in four other lifetimes.

ME: We have? You're kidding! How did it go?

HIM: The usual. Love, hate, love, hate. . . . We find each other irresistible, but then something happens. . . . I never understand what . . . and I begin to sulk and stare out the window into the middle distance—contemplating the assorted seasonal precipitation, the mist, the rain—

ME: This is starting to sound more and more familiar . . .

HIM: So where do you want to go on our astral date?

ME: Well, what is there to do here? Does the astral plane have restaurants and movies?

HIM: There are some restaurants. But I avoid them. The food on the plane is pretty bad. By the way, that's a big joke up here. Every comedian does jokes about plane food.

ME: I see. Very amusing. So! Is there something *you'd* like to do?

HIM: Well, yes. Have sex.

ME: Hey, hey—not so fast. I don't even know you yet.

HIM: Stupid me. Thinking that four other lifetimes *might* count for *something*. Tail end of the 1800s? I was Rodin? You were Camille Claudel? . . . 4 B.C.–1 A.D., I was a pharaoh? You were one of my seventy-four wives?

ME: So we've shared *decades* of horrible pathological behavior!

HIM: Not always. 1920 something. I was F. Scott Fitzgerald. You were Zelda.

ME: I can't think why I'm so hesitant now.

HIM: See—there you go. You're always personalizing everything. I have hated that about you since 1634.

ME: Hey—get your hands off me. Nothing you have said so far has made me fond of you in the least.

HIM: And you have been overreacting for centuries. You never give me a chance.

ME: Okay, okay—tell me about yourself. How do you get along with your mother?

HIM: The recent one I hated. One before that scared me silly. One before that was cold and ignored me. That was the one who turned me into a succubus.

ME: You're . . . a succubus?

HIM: I'm a hyphenate. I'm also an incubus.

ME: My God, I've never *knowingly* dated a succubus *or* an incubus before.

HIM: I think the records show otherwise. I was a succubus-incubus hyphenate in *all* of our previous relationships!

ME: You *were*? Well, the difference is I didn't know. I don't think you ever came right out and said . . .

HIM: Don't I get any points for owning up to the truth? Doesn't the fact that I accept myself now and know my limitations speak to my maturity and evolution? Because, you know, I am not *just* a succubus and an incubus—I also write poetry, I study tai chi—I take a ceramics class.

ME: I'm sorry to have to spoil everything, but . . . and it's not only that I know for sure you're a succubus and an incubus. Although I admit that's not much of a selling point. . . . But how can I ignore the fact that *we* have a centuries-long *horrible* track record together?

HIM: Oh. I see. So that's how it is.

He grows suddenly quiet. He walks to the window and stares out at the rolling fog.

ME: Now who's taking things personally?

HIM: I may be a succubus. I may be an incubus. But dammit, I also have feelings. And I have changed a lot since we were Scott and Zelda. I've had sixty years to think things over . . .

(*He takes out a cigarette, lights up, and exhales mournfully.*)

ME: But I don't want to keep making the same mistake century after century. . . .

(*He exhales dramatically once more, stomps out his cigarette, and begins to walk toward the door.*)

HIM: Fine. No problem. Have it your way. I've been kicked in the heart my whole life. You don't know me. No one really knows me. Sorry I wasted your time.

ME: Hey, look—You came all the way out here. Let's at least have a nice evening. So you're a succubus. So you're an incubus. At least you're working on it. I'm sure things will be better this time. What kind of tea would you like?

As baffling as my astral experiences turned out to be, they still just barely prepared me for the love adviser on this plane that I was about to meet next.

Chapter 13
Looking for Love in All the Wrong Places

THE AD, WHICH WAS ACCOMPANIED BY AN INK DRAWING OF A HEART, said, "Love Channeler has totally new approach for finding and keeping love." It appeared in one of those free publications that they have in stacks on the floors of health food stores, which I routinely peruse.

So I called the number. Because for all the horror stories I've heard about looking for love in the personals ads and at dating services, I have yet to hear even one bad word about love channeling.

"The charge is ninety-five dollars," the assistant who answered the phone explained, "but there might be some additional charges if you require any rituals or shaping." Edward, the channeler, would meditate on me and decide whether I was acceptable. And he would do this without any additional participation or help required from me. "He's very ethical," she advised me. "He doesn't see just everyone." It was kind of exciting and reminded me a little bit of waiting to hear if I got into grad school. Which might be why, two days later, when I still hadn't heard, I started to become slightly agitated.

What if my checkered love record had permanently lowered my psychic GPA? But no. When I called to check, I learned that I had in fact been accepted, and an appointment was set up for the following Monday. I was to bring a ninety-minute tape with me so

I could take home a copy of the proceedings. This came as a big relief because I had been trying to figure out a discreet way to smuggle a tape recorder into the session. Which led me directly to a question I had never before faced in my life: What exactly do you wear to see the Love Channeler? Do you dress up like you would for a date . . . so the love channeler will see you as a likely candidate for love? Or should you be thinking, as I already was to myself, "What the hell is a love channeler, and should I be worried that someone who would call himself that might be dangerous? In which case, wouldn't I be better served by making a wardrobe choice that might give the impression of a woman who occasionally liked to let her fists do the talking?" I decided pants, boots, and a sleeveless shirt to showcase my brand-new biceps, hopefully covering both bases at the same time, like Linda Hamilton did in *Terminator II*.

On the drive over to that part of town, as the streets and the buildings on them became increasingly rundown looking, my brain was racing around in my head like a speed skater. I was genuinely nervous. That's the odd dilemma I always face when I find these peculiar listings in eccentric newspapers. The eventual pursuit of them winds up with me alone, possibly in some rundown building in a questionable part of town with a guy who could be in reality John Wayne Gacy—after all, he had a nice little side profession going as a clown. I would have seen his ad, thought it was funny, called him up, and asked him for an interview.

That's what I was thinking as I tried not to be bothered by the fact that the Love Channeler's apartment house was covered with rust stains and looked like a cheap motel. Hey! It wasn't *his* fault. He wasn't with building maintenance. And he's probably too filled with love himself to have such petty concerns. And look! The people in the next apartment have potted geraniums! And there went a very nice man with a big, friendly golden retriever! He wouldn't live next door to someone that he thought was an ax murderer, would he? Of course not!

So I boldly knocked on the door of apartment 13 (So what? It didn't bother me because I am not *that* stupid, am I?). A large, pale white man in his early fifties dressed in a Snoopy T-shirt answered the door. He had graying hair, cut in the manner of Captain Kangaroo. Smiling, he beckoned me to enter what appeared to be a completely dark apartment. On a bright, sunny morning at ten A.M. this was not a comforting detail. But okay—of course he's going to invite me in! I called *him*." I entered slowly, gazing down at the single lit candle on a coffee table in the center of the cluttered living room. All the windows were closed, blinds and curtains drawn, shades pulled down. There was harp music playing on the stereo.

As my eyes grew accustomed to the place, Edward gestured for me to have a seat on one of the two large couches that dominated the room. Lined along the back of each were many, many stuffed animals. Teddy bears. Kermit the Frog. Strawberry Shortcake. My Little Pony. "Oh! Do you have kids?" I asked, hoping to bond. "No," he answered. This was not the answer I was hoping for.

"You seem nervous," he said to me. "Would it make you feel better if I left the door open?" "YES!" I replied, with entirely too much enthusiasm. "That would be great!" Nothing wrong with a little fresh air! Plus, just on the outside chance that Edward wasn't successful in his attempts to channel me love and began to grow morose and decide that he had no choice but to bury me alive, maybe that nice man with the golden retriever would hear my strangled cries before the coffin was nailed all the way shut.

"Why do you have so many stuffed animals around?" I finally could not keep from asking. "I just really love animals," he replied, "and you can't keep them at this apartment." Which made me feel somewhat relieved. An animal lover!! Except for the fact that it didn't really explain the presence of Raggedy Ann or Strawberry Shortcake.

Seated on the couch opposite me, Edward explained that I was going to be advised by two sources. Because he was going to channel Shontee—a future incarnation of himself who lived anywhere from a quarter to a half million years in the future. "In fact, there are several Shontees that speak to me from this period," he elaborated. Edward first came to know Shontee during a long, lonely drive to Bakersfield about ten years ago when he began to hear this other person talking to him from somewhere. "Like most people, I was brought up in a traditional Western thing where if you talk to yourself, then you're nuts," he explained. I began to play devil's advocate as I searched desperately for some signs of normal behavior to help me feel relaxed. "Well," I offered, "lots of people hear their own thoughts as a voice in their head. I do that." "I guess I'm more traditional than most. I was concerned that maybe I was losing my mind," Edward sighed.

Of course, soon enough he realized that he wasn't losing a mind, he was gaining an entity. "It opened up a lot of dynamics of existence to me. With Shontee's guidance I am able to help shape things for people," he explained, as he officially began the session by asking me a lot of personal questions about my love life: Do I have a lot of boyfriends? Do I date much? How much? Which seemed very intrusive—why did I want to tell Captain Kangaroo about my personal life? Then I remembered he was, after all, the Love Channeler.

"Do many men come on to you?" he continued. "You seem like an attractive woman. Attractive enough for men to come on to you. I mean, you're not Sophia Loren or anything, but you're certainly not a dog either." He was delicately analyzing my problem. "In your current state is there anything blocking you from meeting men?" he asked. "Like do you have an angry roommate or a possessive neighbor who threatens people with a gun?" At this point, I felt it would not be a bad thing to let him know that I did have four big protective dogs on the premises at all times. (Okay, only three are big . . . but that guy from a quarter of a million years in the future could break it to him.)

"What I am going to do now," he said, "is channel Shontee, and we'll start playing what I call musical chairs. I'll go back and forth. . . ." He patted the spot next to him on the couch—indicating that I should sit there. Then he asked me to unbutton the top button of my blouse.

"I'm going to put my hand on your heart chakra," he said, "but don't be scared. I'm not going to grab you." I've had plenty of therapy in my day, but this was the first time I'd had a counselor ask to reach inside my shirt. Well, maybe a camp counselor. Cautiously, I did as he asked. His hand was slightly moist. But this was the least of my issues, since seconds later Shontee made a first appearance. He differed from Edward in that he spoke with the kind of faintly Indian accent that all channeled entities from the *ancient* world seem to have who do not speak with that Renaissance Faire, Irish/English brogue. What a surprise to learn that people a half million years in the future will be speaking this way, too. So much for Esperanto.

So there we were, just the three of us . . . me and both of him, one of them with a hand in my shirt.

"Where does Shontee live?" I asked. "Is he a United States citizen of the future?" "You have a very curious mind. I like that," Edward answered, at which point all hell broke loose as Edward and Shontee began to argue with each other. Leave it to me to be causing trouble a quarter of a million years in the future.

"She seems kind of cool and relaxed," said Edward. "I am telling you, there is a lot of torment," Shontee begged to differ, explaining that he sensed deep within me a lonely little girl-child who wanted love. Apparently Shontee also knew the next incarnation of John Bradshaw.

Edward wasn't convinced. Shontee argued that Edward was blocking his feelings toward me. Perhaps because he was afraid of feeling protective and caring toward me. "I don't usually have that problem with clients," said Edward, frankly puzzled.

"Maybe you're nervous because you know I'm nervous," I suggested, still trying to make things rational. He thought about this. "Only in the beginning," Edward said. "I was walking on eggshells then. You know—the door open and all—but no, *now* I am not feeling you because I can sense how much you want love."

As he spoke, I looked over his shoulder into the eyes of Raggedy Ann and Andy, perched next to an exercycle that had no seat. I had *no* idea where this was headed. "You need to step back, Edward," Shontee interrupted. "You get too involved with your clients."

Silently I thanked him, although I was beginning to grow concerned that only half of this team *liked* me.

Shontee wanted to focus on the pain he sensed I had experienced in my love life. He felt that I must strive for more balance.

"Do you have any questions for Shontee?" Edward asked me.

Only one question came to my mind right off the bat, but I was too embarrassed to ask Shontee what happened to the seat from that exercycle.

It was just as well. Time was running out, and Edward wanted to present me with a choice of solutions he could offer to my dilemma.

"I could develop your inner power to control men," he began. "I do a lot of ritualistic work with people. But before I did any with you I would check with Shontee to make sure that kind of power wouldn't conflict with the little girl inside you. Maybe the little girl could have dolls, okay? In other words, the doll could be like a man, you know what I'm saying?" Actually, I didn't. Which may be why it didn't seem like a very good option.

Which brought us to "drumming"—the tool by which Edward felt he was able to "shape" things. If there was someone I was interested in being with, I could bring in a photo and Edward would meditate on it. "And then do some drumming, and afterward I'll call up your answering machine and leave a message about what went down," he offered. Cost to me: a relative bargain at only seventy-five dollars. But that didn't ring a bell with me either. So we proceeded to option three. "The last thing I could do is make you what I call a stallion clip," he explained. "It's basically made from horsehairs and a few secret ingredients." Perhaps mercifully, he would not disclose what those secret ingredients were. But this seemed like it might be the ticket. Not that a ticket seemed like a particular good idea at this point. But I was thinking, "Well, I've come this far. What the hell. I need a way to end this piece."

So I ordered one stallion clip. Cost to me: $95, which hopefully I can write off on my taxes. Shontee didn't say anything, but Edward thought I made the right choice.

"One of the things I've noticed about you is an intensity in your eyes," he said, "and horses are very seeing people. Basically this 'charm,' for want of a better word, would stimulate all your chakras and allow you to bring in any person that you are looking at." Kind of like Puck in *A Midsummer Night's Dream,* I thought. And we know how well that worked out for him.

So Edward agreed to make me a custom stallion clip that very evening, complete with personalized incantation. "I see you as a hot, passionate woman who is going to waste" were his parting words to me. And as I drove home, I debated whether there was a compliment hidden in there, or if the operative thought was "going to waste."

By the time I got home, there was a message waiting on my answering machine. "I forgot to tell you," said Edward, "that the stallion clip is worn in the 'Triangle of Venus.' You clip it into your pubic hair. Then you must remember to look deep into the eyes of anyone you want to attract. Because the way the magic works is it transfers the energy between your legs through your eyes." The clip was assembled and ready for me, he went on, and I could pick it up the following morning.

Considering how quickly he made it, I guessed he must have had a big bowl of those secret ingredients on hand at all times like they do at . . . oh, say, KFC.

When I returned the next day, Edward greeted me with that extra measure of friendliness a businessman reserves for a good repeat customer. He looked rested and snappy in his "Strawberry Shortcake and Friends" T-shirt, as he handed me an envelope with a poem in handwriting on the back. Inside were a number of white horsehairs shoved into the end of what looked more or less like a roach clip. Edward told me that before I attached it ("hairs down"), I was to chant the following incantation three times. Each time I was to say it louder and more heartfelt than the previous time. It went:

> *When this clip I wear,*
> *arousal and great passion arises in*
> *any eyes I stare.*
> *Like the Great Stallion, lusty and strong*
> *between my legs and in my eyes I summon*
> *those to give themselves to me,*
> *and to me belong.*

"I summon *those* to give *themselves* to me. . . ." Hmm. An interesting if puzzling pronoun assortment, that was for sure. But Edward was excited. He had testimonials from satisfied previous stallion clip users. A fat woman got so much attention from the men who had previously ignored her where she worked that they were literally hurling telephone numbers her way. She was lucky to have gotten out of there alive.

"Have a good time with it," Edward said to me, "and call me to let me know about the exciting things that happen." I said I would. And as a gesture of my own good will, I decided to offer a little advice in return.

"If you're going to do any exercycling," I said as I walked out the door, "be sure to get yourself a seat first." And I was on my way. Ready and waiting for *those* to give themselves to me.

Over the course of the next few days I wore that silly thing to a play, a bar, a restaurant, a business meeting, and a birthday party. Cynical as I am, I was secretly kind of hoping that something unexpectedly magical might happen, and out of the blue *those* would suddenly give themselves to me and to me belong—whatever that meant. And when I look back on it, maybe they did.

No, the Love Channeler didn't bring any love. But maybe the magical part was that he also didn't strangle me and leave my poor lifeless body in a shallow grave somewhere on the outskirts of town. Or dismember me and put my body parts into a wood chipper and then use the sawdust to stuff a bunch of stuffed animals.

Though come to think of it, I would have liked to be a fly on the wall at that autopsy when the forensics experts and the police began to debate why I seemed to have horsehairs in my underwear.

Chapter 14
Learning to Live a Lie

THE IDEA OF BEING ABLE TO ORDER UP NEW BODY PARTS IS AN IRRE-sistible one. I have several friends who got breast implants, and in each case it was because they felt the men in their lives would pre-fer it. This the men in question vehemently denied at the time, although none of them stood in the way of the planned surgery.

And now they all seem to enjoy the results. I have never met a woman who preferred a toupee to baldness, but men seem to have no problem acclimating to fake boobs.

It was interesting to watch the transformation of my newly chested friends. They went from being modest and flat chested to wearing those things like they were war medals. Whereas the women I know who were *born* with big breasts underplay them to such an extent you rarely notice they even *have* breasts, my newly surgeried friends suddenly seemed to be *all* breasts. It was hard to remember they had faces.

I liked the idea of suddenly being permitted to acquire more desirable physical attributes. It *seemed* like a ticket to instant beauty, instant power, instant Love!!

Not nearly so much fun to contemplate is the idea of having someone open up your actual breasts and insert plastic sacks full of whatever the acceptable petroleum product of the moment happens to be. Nor is it much fun to turn a blind eye to the oft-discussed medical complications.

Which I guess is the reason I started reading those ads for "breast enhancers" in the back of women's magazines. "The most exciting advancement in body fashion" is what the ad for one said. I became aware that there were two types for sale. One from a company called Curves. And one from the legendary Fredericks of Hollywood. Both cost about $150 plus shipping and handling. In look and feel both were reminiscent of the material used to make surgical breast-implant sacks. Only these sacks are placed inside the *bra* instead of inside the skin. "Internal insertion of Curves will result in severe body injury," cautions the manual, causing me to pull back from the incision I was about to make with the grapefruit knife. But I'm getting ahead of myself.

I had one previous close encounter with this product when I met a sales rep for the Curves company at an Infomercial convention. I had just finished interviewing the Juiceman and was on the verge of buying a juicer, and I was holding a free sample of a perfume guaranteed to make me irresistible, when a balding, stoop-shouldered man approached me bearing a handsome gold and black box containing two disembodied, flesh-colored breasts, each in its own nesting area. I gasped. I had never encountered a box of breasts before. The salesman explained to me that they were going to be the next really big thing in women's fashion accessories. Right off the bat I suspected they weren't meant to be worn in your hair.

The salesman proudly pointed to the transparent but relatively lifelike 3-D nipple that rested on top of the breast mound. He repeated the company line, which I've since encountered in the product literature. "They look, feel, even bounce like real breast tissue." "If you wear a padded bra," he went on, "while you're hugging or dancing with someone, or if someone brushes up against you accidentally, the other person would be able to tell immediately that your breasts are not the real you. That could be very embarrassing." True enough, I suppose. Who needs that kind of embarrassment? But wait just a second . . .

"Okay, let me get this straight," I said to the sales rep. "I'm hugging a guy, and he believes that my voluminous breasts are the real me because after all they look and feel like real breast tissue. And, even more impressive, I appear to be excited because after all they come with erect nipples. So far so good. But then one thing leads to another and we begin to make out. And he reaches into my bra . . . and *then what*???? Because maybe a padded bra causes one kind of an embarrassing moment, but for God's sake what the hell kind of a fiendish nightmare have I stepped into now?"

To which the sales rep responded coolly, "Well, before you got to that point you would excuse yourself and go to the bathroom." "And remove my breasts and tuck them into my wallet?" I offered. "Exactly," he replied. "But wait a minute," I said, "won't my beloved notice something is suddenly very different than he expected?" The answer the sales rep gave me was the same one with which the product literature is awash. "Depending on your natural breast size and the type of clothing you are wearing, the compensating effect of removing both your clothing and the Curves may make the change in breast size undetectable to others." Oh, okay. If you say so.

Further along in the same brochure appears a testimonial from a satisfied customer who elaborates further what it is like to live in this parallel universe.

"I have never felt so appealing, so attractive, and so womanly before," says Susan from San Francisco. "I have both sizes, which I alternate depending on my mood." And her biological inconsistencies are apparently of no concern to any of the people who are close to her. "Susan is in a great mood today," they may whisper behind her back. "Even her breasts appear larger!!" or "Poor Susan.

You can tell she's down in the dumps. Her breasts are about half their usual size!"

But never mind. I called and ordered a pair of each of the large breast enhancers, which are advertised as being able to raise your bra size by two cups. And within a week, box after box of fresh breasts began arriving at my door. It was a little alarming. Like presents from Ed Gein.

The only difference between the two brands was that the Fredericks of Hollywood version was a tiny bit larger and instead of the 3-D nipple protrusion featured a lovely airbrushed, carefully shaded 2-D painting of a nipple, complete with chiaroscuro and everything! Perfect for wearing with a see-through bra if one is being observed through a telescope from an adjacent apartment building.

I plunged ahead eagerly into the slightly confounding task of how to mount them naturalistically on my chest. This was not as easy as it first appeared. They rendered a common Wonderbra too tight. And that was all wrong anyway. They can't be worn with a plunging V-neck—because after all, they are objects with edges that become visible. The answer was not to wear a larger bra, because they didn't really fill the larger cup enough. They were too big for a B, too small for a C. What was a girl to do?

Suddenly I was spending all my time in front of a mirror, in profile, playing comparative breast games. In one position they were too Mary Tyler Moore Show, in another, too Barbara Bush. It was becoming impossible to accurately assess what looked more real, or less fake. Because once you cross into that never-never land, it is hard to keep track of what you mean by "real."

My first solution was to wear them with a running bra, the tight material holding them in place and also stretching to accommodate their shape.

And so, newly equipped, I headed to the park with my dogs. It felt, eerily, like my dogs and I were taking my breasts out for a walk. I felt vulnerable and conspicuous. Especially since I had erect nipples, even though I knew they weren't mine. But no one seemed to be reacting to me any differently. As the day wore on, the only thing I continued to be aware of was how sweaty my real breasts were getting, stuffed behind their new cone-shaped barricades. I felt kind of sorry for them.

As the weeks progressed, gradually I became more comfortable with my new chest size, although I noticed no distinct difference in the way people were looking at me or treating me.

What they did provide for me, however, was a brand-new fun party trick. At all female gatherings I could frighten the group by suddenly pulling them out of my shirt.

Which is how I came to learn that one of my actress friends owned a pair to wear to auditions. "They make a tremendous difference," she said. "Suddenly producers who were ignoring me are relating to me as sexy. I mean, I always was. But now for the first time they can see it or something."

"Gee, I'm not noticing any sort of specific difference in the responses I'm getting," I said. "It's your attitude," she said. "You've got to act like you're packing."

She was right, and I knew it. So with her words ringing in my ears, I arranged to spend an experimental Saturday night bar-hopping with my friend Christine. I would act like I was packing (if I could figure out what that meant). And then I would sit back and bask in the results.

When I showed up at her house, all dressed up and ready to go, she looked at me quizzically. "Do you have them on?" she said. "Yes!" I said. Apparently I wasn't acting like I was packing even when I *was* acting like I was packing.

"Do you mind if I fix your bra for you?" she asked me, coming around in back of me and jerking on the bra straps to tighten them a lot. The result was the kind of cavern of cleavage I had never gazed down into from this vantage point in this lifetime. "Wow," I said, "that's a big change." It was horribly uncomfortable, but my breasts were so close to my nose now, I could have put sunglasses on them.

"You have to suffer for fashion," she reminded me. Nothing happened at Bar #1. Or Bar #2. Groups of businessmen checked us out. But they were guys who checked out everyone. They were no particular testimony to my new packing attitude.

At Bar #3, however, I sat next to an attractive guy who flirted with me. He was pleasant, well spoken, and even had a nice sense of humor. He was a polite guy, though, so if he was checking out my brand-new massive cleavage, he was discreet enough about it that I didn't notice.

Which is when I decided to excuse myself and go to the ladies' room to check and see how the team was holding up. This was when I discovered something rather alarming. One of my new auxiliary breasts had slipped from its perch and migrated, all on its own, to a unique location just above my waist. It was still upright, the nipple erect. It was held in place against my abdomen by my leotard top. I was a virtual isosceles triangle of breasts. I was stunned. This was one scenario that was never mentioned in the owner's manual.

Not only were the men I'd talked to genteel enough not to have gawked at my fraudulent breasts, they were also not particularly intrigued by my brand-new vertical row of breasts. Even though the bottom third one had an erect nipple.

That was the last time I ever bothered to go out packing. I gradually returned to wearing my regular breasts—not as flashy but not as likely to relocate without telling me.

Nevertheless, here is my testimonial for the company's next brochure:

> Gentlemen! Thank you! Thank you! Thank you! After wearing your product for a month, miraculously my life did not change at all. I was not mugged, harassed, or assaulted in

any way, and as a resident of Los Angeles, that makes me a statistical rarity! For that I will always be grateful!

Merrill in Malibu

Of course, changing the shape of your body is only one way to try to rechart the course of your destiny. One of the nice things about living in America at this point in time is that there are so many different services available to help you do this. Let your fingers do the walking through the back of almost any magazine these days, and you will encounter a host of telephone numbers designed to connect you to the kind of advice you will need to get started.

Chapter 15
Looking Forward to Disappointment

IT WAS THE DAY BEFORE NEW YEAR'S EVE, AND LIKE EVERY RIGHT-thinking American I was reviewing my previous year's resolutions. I'd broken the one about not watching any more TV movies about a woman who marries a guy who seems to be so nice at first but then suddenly becomes abusive and before long is stalking her. (I watched two.)

I made a valiant effort to keep the one about not taking in any more information about Michael Jackson, Princess Di, or Burt and Loni, but ultimately I had to break that one because my health was at stake. I was always out of stuff to read on the exercycle.

On the bright side, I *did* keep the one about steering clear of psychics and fortune tellers and instead sending the money I would have wasted being regaled by inaccurate tales of my glorious future to the Red Cross.

So, here I was . . . only one day left until I had to renew all my old vows and make a few new ones. I had a little free time. I had a little extra money. I called up a telephone psychic. Okay, I called up *two* telephone psychics. I figured if I was going to pay for false prophecy, I at least needed the security of a second opinion.

I had recently been collecting ads for celebrity-fronted telephone psychic services from the back of women's magazines, and now I was startled to find I had *eight* (count 'em! 8!!) to choose from.

Apparently, becoming a psychic is now one of the most popular occupations in America—especially for that segment of the population who cannot find the right sitcom to be in.

Of course, each and every ad guarantees the answers to all questions regarding love and career. And as I began to contemplate which celebrity I wanted to advise me, I was thinking about how little sense the idea of most celebrity endorsements makes. Even in this burgeoning field where the premise, should you decide to play along with it, is that these are counselors and advisers who can help you make those difficult decisions in your life. So naturally you'd want to talk to the people who have been helping Isabelle Sanford— "Weezie"—star of "The Jeffersons," a show that has been in syndication since I knew what syndication meant. If she doesn't have enough money not to have to resort to this kind of thing by now, what the hell kind of advice has *she* been getting? Or Billy Dee Williams, now fronting the Billy Dee Williams Psychic Readers Network. It opens with a recorded message from Billy Dee himself in which he welcomes you and assures you that he has *personally* gathered the best psychics available. Presumably, these are the wise people who helped him with the suggestion that the best way to iron out his marital problems was to play a little rough.

Then there's MacKenzie Phillips—a brand new entrant and another syndication casualty. And Brigitte Nielsen—famous for having a voluptuous figure and a short, failed marriage to Sylvester Stallone (which at this point makes her one of the majority of women in the greater Los Angeles area). She has taken a slightly different tack with her Witches of Salem network. "If you *like* talking to psychics," her ad says, "you'll *love* talking to witches!!" The day I tried the number, a pre-recorded voice told me to "stay on the line after the beep to hear a list of the *psychics* available right now."

And then there is the most incredible celebrity endorsement of the moment—the Lorena Bobbitt Astrology Network. "The future is IN YOUR HANDS" is what the ad actually says. "Let us help you take control of your future." If *these* are the people who helped her make *her* plans, they certainly earned every penny of their $3.99 a minute when they hatched the idea that made her famous. "Don't say no until you hear the whole thing," they must have said. "It sounds kind of crazy, but I think it just might work."

But I felt I would be doing a disservice to the profession not to try out the giants in the field first. So I decided to consult with one of the disciples of the great spiritual seer, La Toya Jackson—a woman who has year after year demonstrated her special powers by continuing to maintain a high-profile show business career without having to demonstrate any actual talent.

And then, just to make sure I was covering every psychic base available to me, I spoke to someone from the Nabisco of the psychic hotlines—the Psychic Friends Network. Just in case the ability to foretell the future becomes somehow more acute via an association with a singer who at one time actually had some big hits.

I'd never tried a telephone psychic before. Just making the call felt embarrassing. When I finally made the commitment by waiting past the beep, and was put on hold while my personal psychic was being contacted, all I could think about was $3.99 a minute. Numbers were clicking by in front of my eyes at lightning speed, like they do on the meter box of a cab piloted by a driver who assumes you don't know the way to the airport. From the moment my personal psychic got on the phone, I felt like I was talking to a cash register.

But here's what was even weirder: *both* of these psychics forecast the *same thing*. At first neither one of them saw anything much happening for me in January. But then, out of the blue, they each announced that during the second week of the month there would be "love disappointment." The second guy narrowed it down even further. "Probably around the twelfth," he told me.

It didn't occur to me to ask the first guy for additional specifics because it was only after the second guy made the same prediction that it seemed like anything to pay attention to. The second guy thought maybe it was someone introduced to me by friends. He couldn't tell me what Mr. Love Disappointment looked like or what he did for a living. He couldn't give me a name. He only knew that a disappointing sort of a break-up vibe was inevitable around the twelfth.

It took him about five minutes to arrive at this cheery proclamation. And I managed to hustle both guys off the phone before they could ruin February. I figured fifteen to twenty dollars was more than a fair market price to pay for projections of disappointment.

And as I sat alone in my room, after hanging up the phone, with my four dogs staring up at me, I couldn't fail to be surprised that *two* guys—psychic representatives of two *different* screwed-up, frustrated singers—foresaw the *same* event. It made the odds of it happening appear to be a good deal more likely. To say nothing of the fact that all they were really predicting was *disappointment*—not exactly the kind of thing that's in short supply.

At first I was kind of bummed. I'd just as soon not have my disappointment foretold by seers. It's not the kind of thing you want written in the stars. But then something occurred to me. For there to be "love disappointment," there also had to be *love*. And since I didn't have anything *at all* happening in the love arena, a brief but tragic affair didn't sound all that bad.

Now suddenly I started to get excited! If love disappointment was the twelfth, then love had to be around the ninth or the tenth. More chain-smoking narcissists must be headed my way! I didn't have much time! I had to go buy some new clothes, maybe pick up a couple extra ashtrays.

The first week of January *was* very slow, just as predicted. But the lack of activity buoyed my spirits and renewed my optimism!! With any luck at all, disappointment was just around the bend! So I used the down time to clean my house, shop, and stock up on plenty of snacks. I even bought flowers and champagne. It felt kind of like preparing for the arrival of an unfamiliar but attractive houseguest with a very bad reputation. Like Gary Oldman was coming to stay for the weekend. Or Robert Downey Jr. or Keith Richards.

I also used the time to do a great deal of convoluted thinking. Since forewarned is forearmed, I began constructing and deconstructing a million hypothetical scenarios. Possibly, if I did my homework and had my wits about me, I would be able to transform the inevitable disappointment into something more positive. For instance, what if I met this guy and we had some kind of instant attraction (and it was going to *have* to be fairly instant, given the limitations of the timetable) and I told him I had to leave town and couldn't see him for a month? Would I then have *circumvented* the disappointment by moving the affair to a different time frame? Or would the same amount of disappointment still result, only now it would be *because* the guy wasn't willing to wait a month? Or was the way it worked that the disappointment would catch up with me and meet me wherever I was, whatever I happened to be doing, *whenever*.

What would La Toya Jackson have done if this were happening to her?

I woke up Monday morning of the Big Disappointment Week fairly bubbling with anticipation. Even though the only love taking place at my home right then was that my dog Winky began an affair with a stuffed headless seal. (The original seal had a head, but one of my other dogs ripped it off. So I sewed it back up anyway because it had cost me a lot of money. And a good thing I did, too. Because as soon as he saw it, Winky fell head over heels into a love so deep that it did require a face.)

Tuesday the tenth was uneventful. Although it did begin with one of those stressful only-in-Malibu experiences that I guess *could* be construed as love disappointment. I got up early to go buy myself a cup of coffee at the local Starbucks. My plan was to dash in, grab some coffee, and race back to the car. I planned to make no eye contact of any kind because I hadn't proceeded with my customary ablutions and was vaguely aware of the fact that I didn't look much better than a headless seal myself. And there is no way that it would ever have mattered at all, except for the fact that MEL GIBSON was sitting at one of the little tables out front, drinking coffee. Okay, yes, I've had a fantasy about Mel Gibson before. But, unless my memory fails me, I don't think it went: "and one day I'll see him sitting in a small café. And I'll walk in, my hair uncombed, my face all greasy and soiled with old makeup, dressed in grimy sweatpants and an inside-out sweater, and our eyes will meet . . . and he'll quickly look elsewhere because he will think to himself, 'Poor thing. She probably spent the night under a bridge. I wonder if she's dangerous.'"

Yes, it was disappointing, but there was *no* interaction with Mel. So unless even *no* interaction with Mel is a cosmic enough matter for *two* different psychics to pick up on, I have to think this isn't what they meant.

However, later that day several rainstorms blew into Southern California. By Wednesday the eleventh, I had experienced every *other* kind of disappointment known to man. There were power failures and highway closures. There were floods and mudslides. The bridge in the center of the town went out. The stores ran out of food, and no deliveries could be made. Malibu was declared a federal disaster area.

Plus I was fired from a job *and* I caught a cold. So it's not true that *nothing* happened in January. In fact, the only thing that *didn't* happen was *love disappointment*. (Unless I heard wrong, and what they actually said was "flood disappointment.")

The following day was the twelfth, the actual date of *The Prediction*. And I felt a surge of Christmas Eve butterflies-in-the-stomach optimism. There was still enough time for a quick and dirty inappropriate love at first sight. A little passion. A burst of pain. Over and out.

So when a friend invited me to dinner and suggested a restaurant around the corner from the apartment of an old boyfriend, I thought to myself, "Aha! Here is where fate will step in. I'll run into him near the restaurant, our eyes will lock . . . and something bigger than both of us will be unstoppable. A tidal wave will pick me up, carry me along and leave . . . disappointment in its wake."

But even with this added boost in the coincidence department, nothing came into my life that evening except a grilled marinated vegetable plate. Which, now that I think about it, *was* a disappointment. Never order the vegetables at a burger place.

Driving home that evening, I finally did give in and just became disappointed. But looking back, I had learned something valuable from the experience. Next time I want to invest thirty dollars, I will get more for my disappointment dollar if I just go to dinner at Victoria's Station and rent a couple of Merchant Ivory movies instead.

Chapter 16
Getting To I Do

"MEN AND WOMEN IN THE 90S . . . GETTING THE RELATIONSHIP THAT'S RIGHT for YOU," said the blurb in the "Events" column in the back of the *L.A. Weekly.* "A *fun* evening at the Century City Playhouse. Live and Learn as Dr. Pat Allen speaks to singles and couples."

My friend Jennifer felt she had gotten something of value from the several times she had attended. "She teaches you that when you're with a man, you're not supposed to say anything if he drives by the correct freeway offramp, because it hurts their fragile egos," she told me one day. We had just finished a yoga class and were out in front of Starbucks, drying off. "Really?" I said. "But what do you do when they start screaming at you because you saw the exit and let them drive by and didn't *say* anything?" She didn't know. So I decided to go find out for myself.

Inside the lobby of the Century City Playhouse the following Monday night, a smiling man in his sixties with thinning hair gestures toward the darkened auditorium just ahead. Pat Allen is still standing in the lobby chatting with her entourage of sixtyish men, one of whom I have heard is her husband.

In the ladies' room, before things get started, a very enthusiastic repeat customer offers an unsolicited testimonial about how she met her husband using Pat Allen's flirting techniques.

Inside the auditorium there is a good-sized crowd for a rainy Monday night in March: about seventy nicely dressed people, mostly white, in their mid-thirties to early fifties. The men are dressed in sport coats and seem to skew a little older. About forty-three of the group are women.

Moments after I sit down, Dr. George, the guy who handed out the tickets, takes the stage. "I'm your disposable, movable host," he says, asking us to "turn to someone, put out your hand, press the flesh! Be sociable! All right! That's enough! Cut! Are you here for some fun? Get ready! Pat Allen is going to regale you with laughter and dazzle you with her brilliance."

With that buildup, Dr. Allen, a sixtyish woman with a pixie haircut, steps to the microphone as Dr. George takes a powder.

She is dressed in a loose-fitting, drapey, gray suit with the kind of pants that almost look like a long skirt, tastefully accessorized with long sparkly earrings and a sparkly matching belt. She is wearing a pair of reading glasses that she continually puts on and takes off and then puts back on again.

Behind her is a painting of the skyline of Century City, part of the set for a play that performs on this stage the rest of the week. The fact that she is framed by a set makes her appear to be a fictional character in some odd one-woman show by Christopher Durang, which in a way is what she actually is.

"How many of you have either read the books or listened to the tapes or are in some way familiar with Pat Allen?" she asks. A few hands go up. "I want the rest of you to know that you are hereby delegated Pat Allen virgins," she continues, "and you're about to be deflowered of some of your most favorite ideals. You will either love it, or you will be challenged by what is said here this evening."

Right away I am in the second group, because I am always challenged by people who insist on referring to themselves in the third person.

Formerly a self-described "little nebbish Catholic girl from Sioux City, Iowa," Pat Allen is now "a cognitive therapist, a transactional analyst, and a marriage and family counselor." She got her Ph.D. in psychology when she was forty, having put herself through college as a professional accompanist ("you know, that funny little lady who plays when someone sings," she tells me). This seminar, which she's been doing for twenty years, is an outgrowth of her college internship.

"How many people want to be in a relationship?" she asks. Lots of hands go up. "How many people want their ideas respected more than they want their feelings cherished?" More hands go up, tentatively now. I am already stumped. Silly me—I thought having your ideas respected was *part* of having your feelings cherished.

"Who wants both?" she asks. Hands go up again. "*You* are here for that problem," she says. "In an intimate relationship we need a composite of one person who wants to say what they want and one person who wants their feelings tended to. Then we have a complementary exchange of energy. "Giving isn't *feminine* . . . it's *masculine,*" she claims. "Giving *back* is feminine." (Huh? Okay, so a guy gives you something, say a ring . . . and then you give it *back* to him. . . . No, that can't be it. So the guy gives you his *love* and you give him love *back*—but what if you loved him *first* so that his initial giving already *was* giving back? Or are we talking about herpes?)

"Male energy gives and cherishes. Feminine energy receives and respects the person who gives and cherishes," she goes on.

I'm confused. So, say one person says, "I want to move to an unheated cabin in Montana and live like the Unabomber." He should also remember to *cherish* his partner's *feelings* by adding, "Are you okay with that, honey? Anything I can get you while I'm packing? Some Xanax? Some Prozac? Honey? Honey?"

This central assumption leads us to what turns out to be Pat Allen's distinctive contribution to the love seminar genre: the "raise your right hand and repeat after me" pledge. In the course of an hour and a half, she will initiate maybe a dozen or more such pledges. Pat Allen has a formula, a recipe, and a pledge for every common relationship dilemma. Such as "Egg people—the feminine energies in the room! Raise your right hand and repeat after me: I promise on my honor to respect the companion I have chosen even though I know I am smarter and can do it better, so help me, God." Then one for the sperm people—"The masculine energies in the room. Raise your right hand. I promise on my honor to cherish my partner even when she is illogical, irritating, and irrational, so help me, God."

There's one for the Cherished Woman: "I promise on my honor to keep my brilliant, educated, liberated mouth shut when he goes by the correct offramp, so help me, God."

There's also the Male Impotency Pledge: "I promise on my honor never to marry a female friend unless the money is right and I don't want a good sex life, so help me, God." And the Addictive Relationship Pledge: "I promise on my honor that I will never let a magic wand in anywhere it can get in until I talk to its owner about his plans for longevity, continuity, and exclusivity, so help me, God."

Until you are engaged you should "always date three people." If you can't find three people you should "go out and look for them, especially at the airport." "Pretend to be taking a trip—bring a bag and everything." Nothing like the anxiety of air travel to stoke up the need for bonding and permanence in life.

Also, everyone should flirt every day, using the Pat Allen five-second flirt training, which holds that "you cannot look someone in the eye for more than three seconds without making an emotional impression." So you aim for five seconds. But there are rules here, too. The woman *signals*. The *man* approaches. The woman is *not* to speak first, "or you risk attracting respect. The first one to speak is left lobe. Male." "Raise your right hand. I promise on my honor I will keep my mouth shut when I am trolling as a sexual person and wait until I am spoken to and then respond enthusiastically no matter how stupid the remark, so help me, God."

She is promoting the idea of what she calls "the covenant relationship," in which "two people make a spiritual commitment to sacrifice for the good of the team." "Never commit to a human being," she warns. "There are no human beings worth committing to. Commit to a relationship. Raise your right hand. I promise on my honor to accept that which I don't approve of and to do my half to make this commitment work, so help me, God."

A person without a right hand would have a lot of trouble with this class.

Now it's time for audience questions, which we'd put into a bucket when we first came in. Or we have the option of just hopping up on stage with Dr. Allen and helping her hone her budding talk-show skills. Which is what a pretty blond woman with blunt-cut hair and rimless glasses does. She is wearing a thigh-length, belted, black leather jacket and she tells us she is forty. "Have we seen each other before?" Pat Allen asks her. "No," the woman tells her. "A virgin! A Pat Allen virgin," says Dr. Allen gleefully.

Her problem, as she explains it to us, is that she was seeing a guy but he said he needed time to think about things and now it's six weeks later. She's wondering what, if anything, she should do now. And as it turns out, Pat Allen has a whole set of theorems on hand to cover this circumstance.

"How many of you women have had a 'space-walk-talk'?" she asks the group, removing her reading glasses. "As in 'I need space. I'm gonna walk. But we can talk'?" When a guy takes a space-walk-talk, they require eight weeks of ruminating. Back and forth from one lobe to the other. Think. Feel. Think. Feel. Think. Feel. It may take him eight weeks to realize that you're gone. If he calls in a month, he's mad about you. If he calls in six weeks, he's thinking seriously. If he calls in eight weeks, he's waited till the last moment.

If he doesn't call after eight weeks, it's over. Raise your right hand. On my honor I promise that if he takes a space-walk-talk, I'll mark off eight weeks on my calendar. And then when he calls, I'll raise the ante. If we were dating, I'll require a commitment. If we were committed, I'll require a wedding date. But I will never ever take him back at the same level at which he left, so help me, God." There's more. While you're waiting, "change the answering machine message to a male voice. If he calls to hear your voice on your machine, it can *keep him away* because it gives him an oxytocin hit." Dr. Allen advises women to "keep 'em crossed" until a relationship has turned into a commitment.

She pauses for a moment to review her notes and her glasses fall off her nose. She stoops to retrieve them. "These are Featherweight Lenscrafters," she says. "I drove over them with my car." "Maybe that's why they don't fit," yells the guy in front of me. (Raise your right hand. I promise on my honor that if I leave my glasses lying in the driveway, I will not complain when someone drives over them with a car, so help me, God.)

Her reading glasses back on her face, she reaches into her red plastic question bucket and . . . pulls out *my question!* "I hear that your husband works for you," I have written. "Which one of you is the sperm, and which one is the egg?" "Good question. There you go. Fine. Good question," she says, a teeny bit defensively. "I'd want to know who I was getting my advice from, too. If I can't live my way, then why listen to me? Right? I wouldn't, either. How many people think I'm the sperm when I go home? Not true. I have to remember to leave Pat Allen *here*.

"He's the masculine and I'm the feminine," she goes on, "although we're both very androgynous. I call him my John Malkovich . . . but I am so grateful because if you think it's easy for a sixty-one-year-old bag to get someone to make love to her, you've got another think coming."

Not exactly the kind of inspirational message of high self-esteem I want to hear from a guru. But at least she wasn't forcing any getting-to-know-you exercises on us. "I make more money than he does," she tells the group, "and way back when we were first engaged, I thought I was 'PAT ALLEN'—we were living together, and I smarted off to him over the phone. I got back to the house, and there was no sign of him. He walked. And you know what I got from that? If I don't watch my mouth, I am going to lose the best thing I've ever had, and I've been married *four times*."

After the seminar when she has a minute, before her little entourage of sixtyish men envelops her and sweeps her into the night, she elaborates a little. "At nineteen I married a nice German boy, a football coach. We did fifteen years, and four girls later he left. Then I did a short one with a cowboy—I married the Marlboro man. I bought him a Harley and took off 3,500 miles on a trip. Then I married a nice Englishman type; we were more like brother and sister—he helped me raise the kids. Then I did eighteen years of single, and then this darling man came to my seminar"—she nods toward a very pale, gray man wearing coke-bottle glasses and dressed in a light gray suit—"and he watched me for two or three years and finally asked me out and proposed on the first date.

"I was dating a gorgeous Italian at the time—it was never going to go anywhere, but everyone should have an Italian once," she went on.

"Men make decisions about this kind of thing, and I had made a decision," her husband tells me, explaining that he had studied her and decided to win her with her own rules. "I surveyed my kingdom and I was forty-five," he says, sounding like a man who is married to and has been listening to a shrink, "and so I said to her, 'I'd like to make our relationship romantic, and if you're with me in a year, I would like us to get married.'"

And so they did. She taught him how to have a relationship. And now he has one with *her*. Living proof that her system works for at least two people anyway (although I forgot to ask him if he packed his bags and cruised the airport for a while first).

The show wraps up with Dr. George once again taking the stage—this time to pitch a line of Pat Allen products for sale. There are books and videotapes and audiotapes and workbooks. There are future seminars and weekend retreats. And as he reads the price list, she holds up the actual items for sale. He is giving, and she is giving back. I think.

Meanwhile, if you are someone who is unwilling to cruise the airport with empty suitcases, hoping to make five seconds of eye contact with an interesting ticket holder, perhaps you can take comfort in knowing that there are other forms of unconditional love available to you at a moment's notice. All you will need is patience, a backyard, and a tolerance for free-floating clumps of hair.

Chapter 17
Animal Love

ALL THIS PRACTICING ON ASTRAL LOVERS AND CRAZY PEOPLE HAS A practical application. It may just be the warm-up exercise you need to provide you with the full mental freedom it takes to truly jump off the deep end into an involved relationship with a creature who is as close to being like an inhabitant of another planet as any you are likely to meet without first undergoing rigorous training from NASA.

I am referring to living with an animal . . . more specifically, in my experience, a dog. I am so far over the edge in this area that even though I am a vegetarian, I still cook a number of very well-received meat dishes for my four dogs: I pride myself on a certain arroz con pollo with mixed vegetable medley that they really love. I beam with joy as I serve it to them, thinking to myself, "Mmmm. Look how much they love my cooking," momentarily forgetting the fact that when one of them throws up, the other three trip all over themselves to see who can get to it first.

So anxious am I to know everything about how to best serve their needs—since I regard them somewhat like I would a foreign exchange student with almost no academic requirements—that I finally got around to reading that book *The Hidden Life of Dogs*. And I must say that I was underwhelmed. I feel that author Elizabeth Marshall Thomas glossed over or ignored entirely some of the most

important dog-related life issues. Yes, she observed a few dogs se-
lecting mates and dealing with their offspring. Yes, she let them run
around in traffic while she calmly marveled at how they didn't get
hit by cars. But it is I, Merrill Markoe, who can provide a deeper
level of dog understanding because I am the one who lives, Jane
Goodall–like, with them day in and day out, sharing with them my
food, my furniture, and even my bed. Constantly consenting to play
that annoying game in which they bring you a filthy shredded thing
and you have to try to pull it out of their mouth until your hands
bleed, at which point they are reinspired to bring it to you all over
again.

No, I don't let them run around in traffic unencumbered like
Elizabeth Marshall Thomas did. Call me overcontrolling—I don't
want to pay the vet bills. But it is this *constantly observed* life of dogs
that allows me to share with you the following valuable, breakthrough insights to aid in the deepening of love between humans
and animals.

Q. Do dogs live by a code of ethics? Are they spiritual beings?
A. Yes, they most certainly are. Take, for example, what I like to
refer to as "the cookie time incident." Every morning at my house
we all wake up at six. By which I mean that they wake up at 5:45
and begin swatting me in the face and sitting on my head until I
agree to get up also. The reason that we all have to get up so early
is that 6:05 is COOKIE TIME. The way this works is that at 6:00
I open the back door, and all four dogs run out into the yard to
pretend to do their ablutions. Sometimes this lasts thirty seconds or
less. By 6:05 cookie distribution begins. On the day of "the incident," four dogs went out back for the pre-cookie time. But only
three dogs reported, drooling and spinning, at 6:05 for cookie time.
Since it is virtually unheard of for there to be less than perfect attendance at cookie time, I knew that something was amiss. A quick
check of the backyard revealed that my dog Tex, in his haste to get

a good place in line at cookie time, had miscalculated his route and fallen into the pool. My dog Tex is not my smartest dog. He has a really tentative grasp of the obvious. If he were a person, he would be Scott Baio. By the time I got to him, he was panicky and fighting for his life as he did the "doggy magnet"—scrambling ineffectively against the slick wall of pool tiles, although he *can* swim. I quickly pulled him to safety. He was fine. He shook himself off and raced into the house. Seconds later, cookie time resumed with its customary 100 percent attendance. But, upon reflection, what impressed me was this: Moments before, the other three dogs had watched in utter silence as a member of the team fell into the pool and began to drown. They had seen his terror, they had sensed his panic and his anguish. And then, fully comprehending the gravity of the situation, they had looked at one another and thought, "Hey! It's COOKIE TIME!" No one had thought to try to bring the matter to my attention. Not because of any lack of sensitivity, or because they are stupid and self-involved, but because, like all truly evolved creatures, they believe in accentuating the positive in a potentially tough situation. It was cookie time! Life goes on.

Q. Do dogs learn from their mistakes? Is there growth spiritually?
A. Yes. Of course. As proof I offer an example involving my large dog, Lewis. Not too long ago, a gentleman caller came to my home. In his successful attempt to curry my favor (Ah! These things always start out *so* promising . . .), he came bearing not just a bouquet of flowers but also *four* different squeaking vinyl dog toys . . . one for each of my four dogs. For Lewis, it was the squeaking yellow hedgehog with the long turquoise eyelashes and the big garish smile. It was such an attractive toy that Lewis took it into his mouth immediately, squeaked it three or four times, and then swallowed it whole. So what began for Lewis as a joyous celebration of the hedgehog turned quickly into a day of groaning, lying on his back, and refusing to eat.

And so it came to pass that an x ray revealed "an ellipse on the pyloric valve," which turned out to be that smiling hedgehog head with the long turquoise eyelashes. I know this for a fact because when I went to pick Lewis up after his $1,500 surgery, the vet presented me with this macabre souvenir cheerily preserved in a clear-plastic Ziploc bag, looking like some fiendish hors d'oeuvre from a Clive Barker party. So peculiar was the sight of this weird yellow smiling thing to me (plus the fact that it was now worth $1,500) that I decided to award it a place of honor on my top bookshelf (right between my McDonald's McNuggct Buddies and my Nancy Kerrigan bubblegum cards). And that is where it stayed, as far as I knew, until the day, about a month later, when Lewis started groaning again and rolling over on his back again and once again refused to eat. Yes, there was another "ellipse on the pyloric valve." And yes, there was another $1,500 worth of surgery, and yes . . . the hedgehog head was missing from its place on the top bookshelf.

At first I was exasperated, until it occurred to me that Lewis had had the courage to get *back* on the horse that threw him—an act of sheer guts for which he deserved to be commended. When I had that ghoulish head presented to me in yet another Ziploc bag, even though Lewis was groggy from the anesthesia and struggling with a belly full of brand-new stitches, he *still* raised himself up on his two hind feet and parted his lips in an attempt to take that decapitated hedgehog head and place it back in his open mouth. And I like to believe that this is *not* because he learned *absolutely nothing* and was going to swallow it a *third* time but because he . . . uh . . . wanted to remind me to throw that damn thing into the garbage. Which is exactly what I did.

Q. *Are dogs creative?*
A. Oh, my God, yes. Once again, the remarkable Lewis must serve as an excellent example of just how creative they can be. Each and every morning, at about 11:15, I hear a very particular kind of clip-

clop-clip-clop. It is a light step, almost a dance. And it has a particular meaning; it means only one thing. It means, "Here comes Lewis with the toilet paper roll." Even though he has been instructed, on a daily basis, that he is not to remove it from the bathroom, his tremendous need to be creative overrides his sense of right and wrong. First he goes to the far end of the house and removes the cardboard center, not unlike the way a chef would pit an olive. Then he gleefully tears the paper into thousands of tiny pieces until my living room area is evenly coated with a wintry pastiche of shredded tissue so lovely that it looks like a New England morning after a light dusting of snow. It is a picturesque tableau to rival any assembled by Martha Stewart. And Lewis is usually reveling in its beauty by the time I catch up to him with the vacuum cleaner.

Q. *Are dogs loyal to just anyone, or are they discriminating, selective, and do they have incredibly good taste? I mean, do they really love YOU?*
A. As it turns out, they are selective and have incredibly good taste, as I will illustrate with the almost fairy-tale–like story of how my dog Bo came to be *my* dog Bo. I met Bo because Lewis and I used to go for walks by Bo's residence of origin, about a mile from my own home.

I guess the sight of Lewis dragging my jerking, flailing body along as though I were a water skier looked like the kind of fun you couldn't pass up, because Bo began jumping his fence in order to join us. Eventually, we would all wind up back at my place, where I would have him in for a drink and a cookie, and then I would drive him back home. Before long, he began appearing on my doorstep and would bark until I let him in. I would greet him, he would come in for a minute, and then I would drive him home. When I spoke with his family about the predicament, they admonished me for letting him inside. So I went to some expense to get railroad ties wedged in the space under my front fence where Bo was making his entrance. But by now, Bo had been tantalized by the contrast in dog-standard-of-living (DSOL) in our two homes. At his place he was limited to the garage and the yard. At *my* place, a virtual doggy nirvana!! Dogs on the furniture! Dogs on the bed! Bones and filthy, dopey dog toys strewn over every inch of the floor!! Arroz con pollo with vegetable medley served daily!! And cookie time at six A.M.!!!!

So, with the determination of a crack addict, Bo began scaling my eight-foot wooden back fence and coming in the doggy door at the back of my house. I would hear a crash in the middle of the night or at six A.M. I would freak over the idea of a burglar. And then Bo would appear on my bed, ecstatically happy to see me. For the next six or eight months, Bo kept on scaling my fence. I kept driving him home. But as happens with so many love affairs I have had, I got really sick of all the driving. And since his legal guardians weren't helping at all, I began to let him spend the night. Every three or four days I would receive a call from the officious owner, who would say, "Merrill . . . we'd kind of like a visit from our dog." But by now, much as it happened with the Montagues and the Capulets, the tension between the two families was building. It was only aggravated by the humiliation Bo's owners must have been feeling about being in the unlikely situation of having their dog *leave them*. Not too long after that, they moved to a house without a yard. And the rest, as they say, is history. It is the moving story of a dog who picked himself up by his bootstraps and transcended his socioeconomic restraints in a brave and successful attempt to find true love, an expanded sense of self, and a really easygoing, disorganized owner.

And so we see that dogs are truly the most remarkable of God's creatures: creative, spiritual, intelligent, sensitive, discriminating. Of course, some mysteries remain unanswered. For instance, the reason creative, spiritual, discriminating beings would eat their own puke. But I will let others answer that question because some things I would rather not think about.

Q. *Do dogs experience romantic love?*
A. Everyone remembers their first love. It is a very special and yet in some ways frightening time. Suddenly there is a whole range of new and powerful feelings. Which is why, when I first observed my smallest dog, Winky, in the throes of a continuous passionate entanglement with my dog-shaped bedroom slipper (who among us can claim to have chosen wisely that first mind-boggling time), I felt that some kind of a parental counseling session was in order. So I lifted him up from where he was stationed in the kitchen doing what he is usually doing—moving slowly from one side of the room to the other, licking the floor—and set him down on the couch with me for a little chat.

ME: Winky, Winky, oh, Winky . . .
W: Yes?
ME: You are getting to be a big boy now . . . not big in physical stature because genetically you are some sort of a Shih Tzu . . . but in the bigger sense . . .
W: What's your point exactly? I'd like to get back to licking the floor.
ME: Well, lately I couldn't help but notice that you are having your first intimate relationship, which to you probably feels very intense, very serious. . . . Please stop licking the couch like that. You're making saliva spots.
W: There is some cheese DNA here on the back cushions.
ME: My point is that when someone, in this case, you, has very strong positive feelings of attachment, like you seem to be having for that slipper of mine, it is an emotion we like to call "love." Which is why, for example, I say, "I *love* you."
W: Is it time for dinner yet?
ME: No, it's nine in the morning.
W: And what time is dinner?
ME: About five, five-thirty. About eight hours from now.

w: *Eight hours???* You're joking. I thought you just said you love me, or was that just more empty rhetoric?

ME: Forget about that for just a moment. I want to talk to you about this very special time in your life, because there are certain dangers, certain pitfalls that perhaps I can help you avoid . . .

w: Eight hours? Isn't that cruel? If I called the humane society, wouldn't they threaten to take me away?

ME: According to veterinary charts and the American Kennel Club, you are just about double your appropriate weight.

w: Oh, but you're perfect. You open the refrigerator door about sixty times a day. You're *always* eating.

ME: Okay, okay. Listen to me for a minute.

w: That's seven minutes to me.

ME: Love can be a very powerful experience. You may find yourself awash in feelings you've never had. . . . When I was a girl of about fourteen. . . . Though now that I think back, perhaps the most intense first love hit when I was in my twenties . . .

w: You can't begin to compare that primitive situation to the one I have with your slipper.

ME: That's exactly my point. The first time it hits you, you don't understand that chemistry and love are not exactly the same thing.

w: You just don't like to *share* anything, do you? Just like with the food portions.

ME: *I* don't like to share? You guys share *everything* with me. Every room in my house, every piece of furniture . . .

w: This is just the way you were acting when Lewis was dating the couch. Suddenly the battle lines are drawn . . .

ME: This isn't about battle lines. Lewis totally wrecked that couch. I was concerned that Lewis was a batterer. I am pleased to see at least that you are far gentler with my slipper . . .

w: You can't compare Lewis and the couch to me and the slipper. Two totally different kinds of relationships.

ME: You're the one who made the comparison. The point that *I* wanted to make is that, as with Lewis and the couch, these things don't always end happily. Lewis destroyed that couch; I had to have it hauled away . . . and that's the way it *is* with love. A lot of times one party gets hurt.

W: Well, I knew he was playing with fire. How stupid do you have to be to get sexually involved with a *couch*???

ME: Anyway, I just wanted to caution you to go slowly. Don't rush things. Take your time. If there's anything I've learned in life it's that there's no good side to romantic obsession.

W: Eight hours *must* be up by now. Let's go get something to eat.

Q. Should you introduce your dog to your astral lover?
A. Not right away. It might be upsetting for them both. Plus, your dog has enough imaginary problems without having to take on any of yours.

Chapter 18
The Pet Psychic Cometh

IT IS THE DREAM OF EVERY FANATICAL PET OWNER THAT THEY WOULD one day be able to converse more fully with their dog, cat, or guppy. Well, maybe not so much their guppy because it's not a good idea to find out the real feelings of a creature who eats its own young. In fact, almost every case might really be a perfect example of the old "Be careful what you wish for" warning. Because it has occurred to me, on more than one occasion, that wordless whining and whimpering under the dining-room table might be preferable to a clear, deep voice, coming from someplace down around your ankles, grumbling, "Hey, big shot. Give me part of your dinner. *Now.*"

But I digress. I found the listing for the pet psychic when I was looking through listings for dog trainers to work with my dog Lewis. Lewis weighs about 115 pounds and has what I calmly refer to as "a greeting disorder," which he recently has expanded into a full-blown greeting dysfunction. In other words, when you come to the door of my house, he feels you have not been properly welcomed until you have been knocked over, bruised, and most of your clothing shredded, stained, or soaked through with saliva. This portion of the greetings lasts a minimum of about thirty minutes and is so exuberant it makes Kathie Lee Gifford appear sullen and consumed with regret. But it is only a warmup for the real event, which has turned out to be a room-to-room couch-humping spree that continues for as long as any guest remains in my house. First he does the couch in the living room. Then it's on to the couch in the den. Then back to the couch in the living room. To say that this behavior display is troubling to visitors is to understate.

My first solution was to get all the couches slipcovered with denim. Then I went through a phase where I tried to simply pretend it wasn't happening. That's the hilarious thing about loving members of another species. You try to put up with behavior from them that you would never dream of tolerating from a human being. Imagine if Lewis was my husband, or my son. And I had to explain to my visitors before they came in the door, "Look—I just want to warn you that when you walk in the door, my son is going to jump you and choke you until you pass out. Then he's going to run into the living room and masturbate. But don't be alarmed. It's just his way of saying hello."

So, I was going to hire a trainer. And then I saw the ad that said "holistic methods for your pet's mind, body, and spirit. Telepathic communication. Increase your spiritual and emotional connection with your pet." How could I *not* call?

On the phone, Ceci Towner elaborated a little. She explained that she also worked with flower essences (soothing to the animal's vibrations) and T-touch (a form of animal massage). She requested that I talk to Lewis and tell him that she would be coming, so he would not be surprised or upset.

She arrived wearing a parka and blue jeans and carrying a large tub of dog treats. Oddly enough the dogs felt a certain simpatico with her right away. She had dark hair pulled straight back, and her unmade-up face was very exotic looking in a beautiful but uncomplicated way. With makeup she could have been Cleopatra, Queen of the Nile. Or a princess from Bali. Or Nigeria. Or Sumatra. A good look for a pet psychic, I thought to myself. She was in her late twenties and said she'd been working with animals for about eight years, tuning in to their vibrations and hearing words or seeing pictures in return. She said she would talk back and forth with my dogs until she learned "their truth." "We're all here to teach each other things," she said. It didn't surprise her that she could talk to animals because she also believed that there can be communication with rocks, vegetables, and plants. "Every object in the world has its own diva," she explained. "Like there is even a diva of couches."

I'd never thought of talking to my couch before. But a chat with this particular couch diva would probably have produced some pretty harsh words about Lewis. Who, true to form, began his greetings as soon as Ceci walked in the door and an hour later was showing no sign of slowing. I was quietly thrilled because I was worried he might for some reason act normal, the way the car does when you finally get to the mechanic.

Ceci explains that she will speak with Lewis and find out why he behaves like this. But first she wants to have a brief chat with my other three dogs. So she sits down on the leather chair in the living room and closes her eyes and doesn't speak for a couple of minutes. She is tuning in to Bo, who is seated across the room with his back to her, scratching his ear. "He sees himself as easygoing," she eventually says out loud, "but every once in a while he has to take control." This is true. Bo is of an Australian shepherd mix and herds the other dogs on occasion. He showed her valentines when he thought about me, Ceci tells me. She says he told her his last family ignored him and didn't acknowledge him as his own guy. Also true, although I can't remember if I told her any of this or not. But by the time she is finished communing with Bo, he is seated at her knees, staring up at her intently. "He really likes to talk," she tells me, moving on to Tex, who is behind her, playing rope tug with Lewis. "He doesn't like the water," she tells me. True again. "In another life he almost drowned." Actually, it was in this life. But with his attention span he probably forgot. He mentions something to her about a blond, with dark roots. Later when I call

Cynthia, the brunette who gave Tex to me, she cannot imagine who this hussy might be and is fairly indignant about the fact that she did not get a mention.

Turns out my little dog, Winky, is "a healer." I'm glad to get this news, though I'm not sure I would be comfortable trusting him with anything more serious than a surface wound. Maybe it finally explains why he spends so much time walking from one end of the house to the other, licking the floor. Perhaps it's a form of healing the floor. But now we move on to Lewis, who apparently tells her he thinks I worry too much.

He's here to teach me to lighten up, Ceci says. Lewis feels that one of his purposes is to spread vibes of love (and perhaps picked up from the diva of couches that both of my couches were lonely?).

He tells her he was traumatized by being separated from a small child when he was young and still has some residual anxiety. (Making me think perhaps I have allowed him to watch too much *Oprah*, because he came to live with me when he was six weeks old.)

But more important, Lewis reports to Ceci that he feels I just do not take him seriously enough. "He's not just a big clown," she tells me. "He's also regal and dignified."

It will apparently take Ceci several more sessions to help us work all this stuff out.

As she is leaving, I ask her if I can learn to talk to my dogs myself. "The whole trick," she tells me, "is getting out of your own way. You have to make your mind blank so you can receive what they are saying."

After she goes home I sit down and attempt to continue the discussion. "Lewis," I begin, my mind as blank as I can make it, "what, oh, what is your truth? What are you here to teach me?" The following is as close to an exact transcript of what he said as I can recollect.

LEWIS: I said it before, and I'll say it again. You don't take me seriously enough.

ME: Well, you are not entirely free of blame in this. It's hard to take you seriously when I see you so wrapped up in toilet paper shredding. Or how about that thing where you run from room to room with a box caught on your head? And what the hell do you mean by that couch-humping thing when people come to the house?

L: I guess you've never heard of good old-fashioned hospitality.

ME: That's the opposite of hospitality. People are frightened and repelled.

L: Pardon me for being too emotionally real for your superficial friends. It's been my experience that people are charmed and delighted by everything I do.

ME: That's where you're wrong. You got that idea because I never discipline you. But humping in front of strangers is considered bad behavior. As is jumping on someone as soon as they come in the door.

L: Now I know you're out of your mind. If I only know one thing for sure in this life, it is this: Everyone is incredibly glad to see me.

ME: Well, maybe I'll leave this alone right now. But before I close our discussion, what is the reason for the toilet paper shredding? I've come up with nothing.

L: To remind you that what man hath created is but an illusion. It has no permanence. It's a message about the transitory nature of life.

ME: It is? Really! I am impressed!! I will never again make fun of it. And the box on the head? What amazing thing are you saying with that?

L: Well . . . uh . . . to be honest, that's just kind of a hobby. You ought to try it sometime. It's very relaxing.

ME: I don't know.

L: It's no stupider than riding a bicycle that is going nowhere.

ME: Maybe you're right. Perhaps I will.

And so a new level of understanding was reached as the result of the direct communication I'm under the impression we had. And that room-to-room box thing really *is* relaxing.

Living with the love of an animal companion is a deep and rewarding experience. Yet despite this, most people still yearn for the greater levels of confusion that they can find only through intimate love with a member of their own species. And so they persist in trying to engage in and perfect this more complex form of love. And the more they wander in that direction, the more they find themselves on a path that is both compelling and potentially treacherous.

Chapter 19
Marriage: What the Hell Is Going On Exactly?

ONCE LOVE HAS BEGUN BETWEEN TWO CONSENTING ADULTS, THERE are basically three paths available to them. They are either headed toward marriage, headed toward a breakup, or headed toward marriage *and* one or several breakups.

Marriage is like a badge of accomplishment and completion in a love relationship. Ninety percent of all Americans get married at some point. And this is despite the fact that they know that 50 percent of these marriages will end in the pain and discomfort of divorce. As Ralph Waldo Emerson said, "Is not marriage an open question when it is alleged from the beginning of the world that such as are in the institution wish to get out and such as are out of the institution wish to get in?" Or as I said earlier in the book, love follows the timeless model of my dogs and the car.

Traditionally, marriage involves one man and one woman, an idea our government just reinforced when they refused to pass a bill that would have extended the privileges of marriage to gay couples. It is hard to say why people are so resistant to this idea. It's impossible to imagine that gay couples could make a bigger mess of things than heterosexuals have done. Perhaps it would be in the best interests of the institution of marriage as a whole to just turn it over to the gays and let them refurbish it and gentrify it the way they do deteriorated neighborhoods, and only *after* it has been restored to its former value would heterosexuals be allowed to move in and defile it again.

Meanwhile, marriage continues to be the accepted way for a man and a woman who are in love to make a public statement about their commitment to each other. It is not unlike the way a campaigning politician makes a public statement of his policy intentions. No one really holds either of them to the letter of their words. People only expect them to at least *try* to play along. In the case of marriage, if things go pretty well, the couple will be expected to stay together five or six years. Politicians are only really expected not to flat-out *deny* what they said in the first place.

Bartlett's *Familiar Quotations* is full of inspirational thoughts on the subject of marriage. "Marriage, if one will face the truth, is an evil but a necessary evil," said Menander sometime between his birth in 342 B.C. and his death at age fifty in 292 B.C. I do not know how many marriages he lived through in order to draw this cheery conclusion, or if he rated them successes. But historically, marriage became more and more a necessity of life as the importance of the agrarian society grew. Once our European ancestors settled down to farming, they also paired off for life. Matriarchy diminished, as did the general power of women in society. It is speculated that the plow was responsible, as it was essential for farming and required someone of the size and strength of a man to operate it.

Yet, surprisingly, no one really gives much credence to the notion that today's marital woes might be helped if a little farming was required of all newly married couples. Perhaps community colleges could offer plowing seminars and apartment floors could be retrofitted to accommodate a patch of soil and a small irrigation system. Because, as farming life began to erode, divorce began to rise, and it has been rising ever since.

The definition of romantic love in a marriage has also changed radically along the way, as we see in the traditional childhood rhyme "Clap hands, clap hands! Till Daddy comes home. 'Cause Daddy's got money. And Mommy's got none." Somehow, the fullness of time has made this adorable poem seem a lot less adorable.

Once a couple has decided to marry, they take a first step by becoming engaged. This is not just a public statement of intention but also serves as a testing period to see if anyone is going to chicken out.

The tentative, unnerving texture of this period is addressed in the poem "Engagement Is a Special Time," in which the always edgy Hallmark poets paint a portrait of a couple entering into

> *a time they will treasure*
> *thru laughter and tears*
> *and return to again and again.*
> *Thru a lifetime of sharing and loving and caring*
> *and the best part*
> *"Remembering when."*

Here we sense the feelings of disconnection and hysteria that can cause a couple to experience simultaneous responses of laughter and tears. These are exacerbated as the couple returns again and again to relive this terrifying turning point. And once again, we encounter the shaky emotional landscape typical of the Hallmark poets as they describe the painful inability to experience enjoyment in the now, as the lovers are forced instead to know it only at a later time in the form of "remembering when."

In our culture, an engagement is made official by the gift of jewelry, frequently a diamond ring. This is not true for all cultures, as we see in the Mehinaku, an Amazon tribe of Brazil, who offer the better calculated gift of fish. By giving a gift that has a specific shelf life, the Mehinaku men do not wind up furious and bitter when the engagement comes apart. Because the question of whether the woman should return the fish to the man who gave it is obviously a moot point.

The Mehinaku are a wise and interesting people. They also discourage open displays of romantic love among newlyweds because they believe that excessive thoughts of a loved one can attract snakes, jaguars, and malevolent spirits. This belief not only protects newlyweds but also helps the single Mehinaku people feel better about themselves. Sure, they may be lonely, but at least they have the comfort of knowing that their lives are relatively snake and jaguar free.

In our society, the successful engagement ends in a marriage ceremony. This involves paying for a hall, photographers and videographers, engraved invitations, musicians, limousines, hotel rooms, flowers, champagne, dresses and suits, catered multicourse meals, and very expensive jewelry. Relatives and acquaintances of the bride and the groom are invited to attend the ceremony and expected to purchase expensive presents for the happy couple in question, even if they have done so for each of the two individuals separately in their previous (multiple) marriages. This whole process is designed to be as complex, costly, and emotionally harrowing as it is in order to acquaint the happy couple with the realities of the married life that lies ahead.

Once the wedding is over, trying to make love endure becomes the goal. The idea is to move through time with the object of your affection, locked in a dance of love that is self defining.

So what does make a marriage work? Well, willingness to continue being married is one answer. But not necessarily the only answer or a good definition of the word *work,* as we see in the case reported in the *L.A. Times* regarding "a 71-year-old woman who was arrested after she allegedly doused her husband of more than 30 years with rubbing alcohol and set him on fire for eating a chocolate Easter bunny she saved for herself."

Apparently, simple relationship longevity does not a good marriage make. In the book *The Good Marriage,* by Wallerstein and

Blakeslee we learn that enduring romantic marriages are composed of partners who have idealized each other. "Marriage without fantasy or idealization is dull or dispirited," the authors tell us.

Benjamin Franklin apparently agreed when he said, "Keep your eyes wide open before marriage and half shut afterwards." The Hallmark poets clarify the point further with the poem "This Is a Husband," in which we learn:

> *A husband is a knowing look*
> *a hand within your own*
> *The voice you always want to hear*
> *when you pick up the phone*
> *He sees you when you're at your worst*
> *And loves you anyway . . .*

Not a very rigorous set of specifications, though nonetheless touching and insightful. Oddly enough, "This Is a Wife" is basically the same with a gender modification—and not a description of manual labor as I expected. The poem also accurately describes my relationship to my dogs, even though they are reluctant to talk on the phone. But then, so, too, are many husbands.

What, then, causes a marriage to falter? Well, in *The Good Marriage* we learn that many marriages fail because the husband or wife is unable to successfully separate from his or her family of origin. Marriage requires making a new primary alliance, a trading in of one family tie for another. But thanks to repetition compulsion, we often marry an exact duplicate of the family from which we came. So, of course, this is going to lead to a conflict as the two sets of families war to determine whose job it will now be to continually point out your shortcomings.

Once that barrier has been surmounted, the next task in building a marriage is relinquishing self-centeredness, identifying with the other person, and "building empathy and *we*-ness." About half of the work here involves overcoming sheer gut-level repulsion at the sound of the word *we*-ness.

A long-held axiom of the happily married couple is "Never go to bed angry." This is thought to be a very good idea, even if it does occasionally involve staying up in a murderous rage, stalking around, delirious from lack of sleep, for days if not weeks at a time.

At Long Last: Marriage Day

I was driving home one evening when I heard a radio promotion that caught my interest. "Sunday has been declared Marriage Day," it said. "There will be a huge Marriage Day Pre-Party at the Doubletree Inn, followed by a *historic* two-hour telecast with John Gray, author of *Men Are from Mars, Women Are from Venus*."

So, to pursue my research further, I called and ordered two tickets. I knew of no one who would go with me. But it was way too embarrassing to call and order one ticket for Marriage Day.

I awoke Marriage Day morn filled with the kind of dread I used to feel knowing it was a school day. The man who sold me the tickets told me to be there at twelve-thirty. I got there at twelve-forty and was surprised to see no crowd, no media outside the Doubletree Inn—no indication that a Historic event was taking place inside.

Except for the fact that a woman janitor wielding a dustpan gave me such a hearty greeting—such a *big* "Hello! How *are* you?"— that it appeared someone from management may have had a talk with her.

She pointed straight ahead, toward the closed doors of the Marquis Ballroom. Cautiously, I opened them, not sure what portion of the Huge Marriage Day Pre-Party I would be invading. What I found was a darkened room filled with about forty silent people, sitting in straight-back chairs watching a large-screen satellite feed. If there ever was a huge party, there sure was no sign of it now— not a paper plate or cup, not an empty hors d'oeuvre tray. Not a decoration remnant or a lingering, hungover musician.

I slipped into an empty seat in the back row to watch John Gray, the baby-faced, lima-bean–headed Mars-Venus mogul, address a large group of his devotees in an auditorium somewhere else. He was dressed in a double-breasted suit. Hanging behind him were large blow-ups of his best-selling book covers. His relentless, upbeat cheeriness was a real homage to Kathie Lee Gifford.

Not surprisingly, most of the people in attendance were couples. There were also several groups of three—not a traditional route to making a marriage survive but still preferable to the one O.J. took.

The couple in front of me, dressed in matching fire-engine-red shirts, looked like the fiftysomething version of Fred and Wilma Flintstone. He was portly, with a thick neck and hair trimmed in semicircles above his ears. She had her hair pinned up and her arm around him, nuzzling him supportively every time John Gray said something she thought was true. For instance, when he spoke of how men use their brains differently than women ("when he *feels*, he can't *talk*"), she whispered, "Is that right?" into her husband's ear, snuggled a bit closer, and put her head down on his shoulder. It was hard not to imagine him red-faced and stammering after being informed that she had bought them these tickets. The amazing secret marital manipulation she used to get him into the red shirt and into the car is something I needed to know.

For the first hour of the lecture John Gray delivered his standard Mars-Venus fare—which a woman seated beside me told me she had heard almost verbatim three weeks earlier at the Palladium: "Women need to talk and to be heard. Men need to learn that all they have to do is listen, *not* solve everything. Woman have 'a well' where they store feelings. Men have 'a cave' where they go hide.

Men are a blowtorch. Women are an oven." Sitting there was making me lethargic, even sleepy.

But by contrast, the devoted couples around me were reacting as though they were listening to a Barry White record. A Hispanic man with rimless glasses and a ponytail was rubbing the leg of his chubby, fiftyish wife as she caressed his shoulders.

Eventually, John Gray explained that a contest had been held on America Online. And that the winners of the big Marriage Day contest were coming to the stage to repeat the vows they had written to "inspire couples *for generations to come,*" thus answering the question "Did having a number of best-selling books go to this guy's head or not?"

"I'd like my wife, Bonnie, to come up here, too," he added, beckoning Mrs. Gray—a sensible, pleasant, gray-haired woman in a polka-dot dress, who was welcomed with the great applause that always greets the emperor's wife. She was followed by contest winners Mike and Carol Fussman, two people in their thirties who were so sober and mature in their demeanor they could easily have passed for fifty.

"Now what we're gonna do is give them an opportunity to read their vows," said John Gray, "and as they speak, I am going to feel in my heart similar feelings and I'm going to communicate them to my wife as I look into her eyes. I invite all of you here in the studio and in all the Doubletree Inns around the country to take this time to renew your marriage relationship. So stand up right now . . . ooh, you weren't expecting this, were you?"

Only two couples in the room I am in have the sheer guts to help inspire the generations of the future: a white-haired couple who look like they have come straight from a line-dancing class and a sheepish, pudgy-looking couple in their forties. Wilma looked at Fred, but Fred made no move, staring straight ahead, pretending he didn't hear.

"Now turn to your partner and hold their hands, like Bonnie and I are doing," said John Gray, "and be looking into your partner's

eyes and go back in time to when you were first married and remember the love you felt in your heart. Remember how beautiful
your partner was and how proud you were of them . . ."

Aaah, we are going back now . . . back in time . . . back before a chocolate Easter bunny was as good a reason to set your
husband on fire as any other . . . because *this was at long last the historic part of the telecast*!!

Michael Fussman, in his aviator glasses and dark sport coat,
began to speak: "Dear Carol, I love you because you make my life
complete . . ."

And as the vows were spoken, John Gray looked at his wife
with his sincerity beams up so high that he was virtually glowing
and crackling like a bug zapper. His wife did not seem to mind, but
I wanted to smack him.

"Michael, I love you because you have taught me that true
love can endure all hardship," Carol Fussman read back. And now
I think maybe I *have* learned something from Marriage Day: That
perhaps the most valuable ingredient in a marriage is the ability to
continue to love your husband or wife, even if they have so little
sense of cultural irony that they make you share intimate personal
vows on a stage while John Gray stands behind you beaming his
brains out, hogging the camera like an out-of-control scene-stealing
child star.

Now at last I get it: It's another test. Make it through Marriage Day and dammit, you have yourself a real marriage.

Marriage Part Two

Still not convinced that I had learned everything there was to know
about what makes a marriage work simply from having attended
Marriage Day, I arranged to spend some quality time with the one
happily married couple I know in order to better observe the complex mechanism that makes this way of life work for some people.

My friends agreed to let me live among them for a brief period of time—*brief* being the operative word. It was arranged that I would join them at one o'clock on a balmy Sunday in June.

1:00

Mrs. X answers the door of the spacious California-style home, which is identical in decor to the one Mrs. X had when she was single. Mr. X, when he was single, lived in a room with a bed, a broken chair, and no windows, so there was not much debate as to who would take charge of the decorating in the home they now share. Mrs. X has been careful to include many photos of Mr. X in the decor so he will be reminded that he lives here, too.

2:30

After a beverage offered by Mrs. X and some polite chat, we all board the Xs' fashionable all-terrain vehicle—a necessity for their active, all-terrain lifestyle—all terrains in this case being concrete, asphalt, pavement, *and* cement.

Mrs. X sits in the back seat, beside 1½-year-old Baby X in his baby seat. Mr. X is in charge of the navigational duties. We are headed to something called Universal City Walk, which Mr. X explains to me as "kind of a combination of a shopping mall, an amusement park, and your worst fucking nightmare." We are planning an afternoon of family fun.

2:40

Having parked in a multilevel parking structure, we head out on foot—father carrying a large purse full of survival items, mother carrying the baby. Because he is hauling less weight, Mr. X is the first one to reach the crowded communal gathering area, which is gaily decorated with outsized replicas of things for sale: a giant soda, a huge hat. As we walk, we stop briefly in an area where a constantly shifting crowd of tiny children are watching what appears to be a woman dressed in the colorful mismatched clothing of a derelict. Her face is smeared with unattractive white makeup, but rather than lying in a pool of her own vomit, she is twisting long, cylindrical balloons into odd unidentifiable shapes that resemble certain mutating single-cell life-forms. She holds the children's attention by talking to them. "How did I get this job? If you want to make balloon animals, you have to go to college," I hear her say to a child who appears to be about three, "because that's the only kind of job you can get when you graduate." The tiny children for some reason are amused by this.

3:15

We each must pay a fee of thirty-four dollars to be entitled to the assortment of more significant opportunities for family fun that exist just beyond the turnstiles. So we walk past pretzel carts and popsicle carts . . . until we arrive at an amusement site apparently designed to replicate the look and feel of the critically loathed and publicly shunned movie *Waterworld*. Sadly, the next SEA WAR SPEC-TACULAR will not begin until four-thirty. And so we move on, through endless corridors, as though we are searching for a gate at the airport that will turn out to be located in another terminal. We are trekking, ever trekking, in the beating hot sun. I am reminded of a thousand Sunday afternoon outings with my family as a child. Except by now my father or mother would be screaming at me, my brother, and each other, while the Xs continue unperturbed, understanding that the survival of tedious recreational challenges such as these are the very building blocks in the foundation of the American family.

3:30

We arrive at a ride called Back to the Future. If the ailments listed on a sign that informs us they can be worsened by experiencing this ride are any indication—seizures, back conditions, neck conditions, eye problems, etc.—the future is not going to be a place for the weak. Irritability, irascibility, and ennui, the conditions from which we are suffering, are not listed on the sign. So we get in line, and it is full speed ahead . . . until we are informed that baby cannot be admitted. This is terrible news. But a solution is presented to us by the park employees!! The E.T. ride, which is just around the bend, will be *perfect* for everyone, baby included.

4:00

We head back across yet another landing-strip–sized stretch of concrete—the glare of the reflected sun making us squint. The E.T. ride, we are told, is right down those escalators over there. What we are not told is that "those escalators over there" are four of the longest, steepest covered escalators known to Western civilization. They negotiate an entire hillside, are nearly vertical and so interminable they could almost be considered a ride unto themselves, were it not for the fact that they provide almost no entertainment.

"Are you sure you don't want to just bag it?" Mr. X says to Mrs. X, empathetically. "No, no, I don't want to bag it," she replies, the music from *Ghostbusters* playing eerily behind her. This display of genial good feelings in the face of adversity accomplished, we all continue to escalate ever downward in silence for minutes so long they redefine the entire nature of time. What the park was able to do to make these minutes so slow is a spectacular effect in itself.

4:25

We spot the E.T. ride and approach eagerly, only to be turned away again. Although recommended by the park employees as perfect for everyone including baby, it is in fact off limits to baby.

4:30

We are headed back up the escalators. If we can only learn to be amused by staring straight up into the nostrils of the unhappy people headed downward, we could pretend that this was a ride.

4:50

Back on the endless tarmac to nowhere, the white concrete all around us glaring like slick off-season snow. Maybe we will go to customer relations and demand our money back. There could be some entertainment value in that, we are thinking out loud as we pass by the Flintstone Theatre a second time, and this time . . . it is only ten minutes until the show!!!

A rap song that has managed to work "yabba dabba doo" into its lyrics is playing as we open the faux rock doors that lead into the packed playhouse.

Interestingly, baby X—who had been smiling and patient and relatively amused by the glaring concrete, the beating hot sun, the tedious escalators—now finds proximity to actual pending festivities to be a push too far in some direction. He begins sobbing as we all sit down on one of the many aluminum benches across the aisle from a woman wearing the traditional headdress of her native Middle Eastern country. She is trying in vain to comfort her own weeping child. In fact, children of many nations are suddenly inconsolable as showtime nears.

As the houselights dim, Mr. X is awakened from dozing to see many, many dancers in primary-colored cavewear dancing and lip-synching to songs about Hollywood coming to Bedrock.

By the end of the show, when a fake volcano erupts and small fake fires break out all around us, the audience has experienced a metaphoric feeling of triumph. They know they have transcended personal discomfort, theoretical danger, and infantile entertainment—the three key ingredients to surviving as an American family in the nineties.

"Well, we made it," says Mrs. X proudly, as we gather up everything and prepare to head back to the car. The marriage is intact.

Chapter 20
What the Movies Taught Me

RECENTLY IT OCCURRED TO ME THAT ONE THING I HAVE NEVER DONE is sit down and really study the classic movies about love. I was a TV kid, and when I did go to the movies, it was in search of laughs—which is perhaps an even more futile pursuit, given the state of movies.

So this past weekend I decided I would add this piece to the tattered fabric of my love education.

Longing Rules

I began with *Casablanca,* the movie that has provided our culture with more romantic buzzwords than any other. Apart from the fact that the famous line Ingrid Bergman speaks is "Play it, Sam. Play 'As Time Goes By'" (and *not* "Play it again, Sam"), what first struck me was how no one ever mentions the line that precedes this great classic love moment of the American cinema. Which is when Sam the piano player looks over at her balefully and remarks, "Leave him alone, Miss Ilsa. You're bad luck to him." *And* the renowned "Here's looking at *you,* kid" turns out to be a toast made by the love-besotted Humphrey Bogart only seconds after he and the object of his deep affections have this discussion: "Who are you really?

What did you do before?" he asks. "We said *no questions*" is her reply.

What can we learn from all this? That danger, pain, and ignorance are important ingredients in love.

The coup de grâce comes when Bogart says, "We will always have Paris," as he parts with her for the final time. "I said I would never leave you," she says, choking back tears. "And you never will," he replies, reminding us that longing for what you can't have is bigger, better, and far more romantic than living with anything that you do have.

This also turns out to be the model for the first reel of *Dr. Zhivago* (which is as much as I saw . . .), but *all the way to intermission* the burning desire of Omar Sharif for Julie Christie is more significant than his nice, serviceable marriage to the plucky, well-intended Geraldine Chaplin. Ditto for *The Bridges of Madison County*. One weekend with Clint Eastwood—one slow dance in the kitchen—becomes a bigger deal in the scheme of Meryl Streep's life than the marriage that apparently lasted for decades.

First Love Is Everything

On the teenage love front *Splendor in the Grass* tells the story of two high school students whose love for each other burns so brightly that one of them (the girl, of course) has to be committed to an institution. By the time she gets out, he is happily married to someone else—a teenager who was willing to take a few risks instead of blowing everything like selfish Natalie Wood, who retreated instead into therapy. It looks like the new couple has a pretty good marriage, too, leaving us with the clear message: 1) take time out to get help for your so-called emotional problems and you do so at your own peril, and 2) it is far better to just plunge ahead into the maelstrom of first love than forever live to regret it.

Something similar is at the core of *A Summer Place,* in which Sandra Dee and Troy Donahue (pretending to still be teenagers) fall in love in a landscape of crashing waves, violin crescendos, and divorcing neurotic parents. "I love you so much I ache inside," says Troy, the cleanest young man in America, to the overwrought Sandra Dee. While elsewhere on the island resort her father is saying to Troy's mother, "I love you too much to speak." It was good old-fashioned, searingly painful love everywhere you looked that summer.

Meanwhile, Sandra Dee's disdainful prudish mother dispenses the advice that "You've got to play a man like a fish." (Leaving the intriguing but sadly unanswered question, How exactly does one play a fish?) By the end of the film, despite all kinds of ordeals, the teenagers get married "in front of God and everybody," because, as we must remember, you have to grab that all-important first love and hang on to it. Or a loveless, miserable existence with the wrong person will be your fate.

Of course, the above are examples of sober, level-headed thinking compared to the plotline of *Romeo and Juliet*—two names that have become synonymous with the idea of romantic love. Even though they belong to the stars of a nightmarish story of two pre-teen kids who get married just one day after they meet. After which Juliet returns home to live with her parents, who, of course, have no idea that any of this has happened. But had they known, it would not have been the age factor that upset them, because they have already gone to some trouble to line up a husband for the not-getting-any-younger Juliet. When Juliet learns of this, she is obviously upset, and so she feels she has no choice but to take the most intelligent course of action under the circumstances—she pretends to be dead. This behavior bodes very well for her budding skills as a wife and a problem solver. It's just too bad that she and her teenage husband couldn't have stayed alive and remained married. They certainly would have wound up creating a new record for 911 calls in a given period of time.

Lying Is Good

In *While You Were Sleeping,* the lonely Sandra Bullock decides she is in love with a guy she saves from being crushed by a train, even though she knows nothing at all about him. So while he is hospitalized and in a coma, she embroils herself in all sorts of lies about being his fiancée. She feels she cannot come clean because "his grandmother has a heart condition, and if she finds out. . . ." When coma-boy finally does come to, and is disoriented from head injuries, he gets talked into going ahead with the marriage by a nosy neighbor; neither of them is particularly concerned that he does not know his bride-to-be at all.

Of course, by the actual wedding date Sandra Bullock is forced to confess that she is really in love with coma-boy's brother. (And why wouldn't she be? They met one day when she accidentally slammed his head into the door and bonded later that evening as they slipped and slid into each other on an icy street.) And so we have a touching tale of love that is born of catastrophe and the essential ingredients of love, which are: accident, lying, clumsiness, desperation, and completely delusional thinking.

Don't Rule Out Freaks

Which brings us to my favorite love movie of all time: *Cool As Ice,* starring the one-time immensely famous white rap star of the nineties, Vanilla Ice. The story begins when Vanilla, dressed in his signature backwards baseball cap and leather jacket and sporting a haircut full of more shaved patterns than a miniature golf course, is minding his own business riding along a scenic country road on his colorfully stenciled canary-yellow motorcycle with a number of his homies, when he sees a pretty girl riding her horse behind a picket fence. Naturally, he does what any newly smitten suitor would do under the circumstances. He jumps his motorcycle over the fence so that it lands blocking the trajectory of her galloping horse, causing it to rear up on its hind legs and throw her. Luckily for the sake of their love, this does not sever her cervical spine and paralyze her. Instead, it causes her to yell, "What the hell is wrong with you?" and throw a punch at him before she gets back on her horse and rides away—a gesture that he takes for the declaration of love that it truly is. Watching her with his face arranged in an expression that he is hoping resembles a degree of bemused detachment, Vanilla Ice says to no one in particular: "Yep. Yep. She likes me."

And so it comes to pass that he and his homies are "chilling in the hood" across the street from the teenaged equestrian and her family. One evening Vanilla is out dancing on his front lawn, as is his wont, when he sees the girl having a fight with her current boyfriend. This leads him to speak the words that will one day take their place in the pantheon of classic love-movie lines: "Drop that zero and get with the hero."

By the time he tells her, "It ain't where you're from, it's where you're at," they are in some kind of love. And this is before he saves her skeptic of a father from some crooks who are after him because he (Dad) has a secret past involving the witness protection program.

Obviously, this causes Dad to change his tune when it comes to this Vanilla Ice character. And by the end, when Vanilla pulls up on his motorcycle and says, "Whatcha gonna do now, college girl?" it is okay with everyone that she get on the back and ride off into the sunset with him.

Leaving us with the very same valuable reminder that can be gleaned from Frank Capra's *It Happened One Night*. It is this: Don't be foolish enough to look past that slightly frightening, inarticulate, or intrusive waster who inserts himself into your life, ignoring your protests. Because . . . it could be he will end up not just straightening out all your problems and/or saving the life of your family, but also offering you the kind of love you could never find with a more normal guy.

So, summing up, here is what the great love stories have to teach us:

1. It is important to initially recoil at the sight of the person you are going to marry. The deepest kind of love begins with two people who are repelled by each other.
2. Then it is a good idea to encounter as many insurmountable obstacles as possible. The more nightmarish the disaster, the deeper and truer the blossoming love. Car wrecks, wars, geographical disasters, and political tumult are all excellent situations for true love to grow.
3. The first big sign that really important love is blooming is when slow dancing breaks out in either the kitchen or the living room.
4. The less you know about the object of your desire, the better it is for your romantic future together. From Humphrey Bogart to Sandra Bullock to Vanilla Ice to Romeo and Juliet—most of the really great movie lovers know nothing at all about each other, and like it that way.
5. When in doubt about how to behave once the throes of passion have hit, whenever possible *lie*.
6. Anyone available is never as good as someone you cannot have.

Hmm. Pain, ignorance, lying, insurmountable obstacles. Longing is better than having. Well, how do you like that? Turns out I have been doing everything right all these years.

Which is why when I saw the ad for a course in Divine Love I felt I owed it to myself to find out what this might be.

Chapter 21
Divine Love

TWENTY-FIVE WOMEN AND TEN MEN ARE SITTING IN THE PEWS OF A pretty church in West Los Angeles on this lovely spring evening to hear an ordained Unity minister and student of the Dalai Lama tell us how to find a Soulmate and have a Happy Holy Relationship. There are stained-glass windows and bouquets of fresh flowers and, of course, a table set up with a display of the speaker's books and tapes for sale.

Sadly, there are no snacks for sale. My friend Judy and I have come straight from a very fatiguing yoga class, and we are both starving. And we might not be the only ones with this problem. Looking around at my fellow classmates, I cannot fail to notice that a large percentage of them appear to be . . . well . . . fat. There are at least five who are in the 250- to 300-pound range.

Joan Gattuso, our lecturer, takes the stage dressed in an off-white collarless coat and matching pants. She has medium-length brown hair and is fortysomething or fiftysomething.

"How many people have been working on themselves?" she asks us. Most hands go up. "Oh, I love coming to California," she says. "It's true! It's true!"

And in honor of our cliché California characteristics she wants us to close our eyes, breathe deeply, and bring our energies together as we put aside the activities of the day and "move into the space of our hearts as I share with you . . . 'The Knowing.'"

It sounds familiar. I get an image of a grinning Jack Nicholson hacking down a door with an ax. Oh, right. That was *The Shining*. Joan Gattuso has quite a different message to share than did Stephen King.

The message of her life, she says, is that "there is a way to live and love in the universe that is truly transformational." There are *Limited Special Relationships* and then there are *Holy Relationships*. Limited Special Relationships involve "loving someone for the *wrong reasons*. Such as what they can *do* for us." People make the mistake of using these relationships to try and complete themselves. But the reason everyone loved the movie *Sleepless in Seattle* is that it reminded them that there IS someone REALLY RIGHT FOR THEM.

(Everyone except me . . . someone who did not only *not* love *Sleepless in Seattle* but who was reminded by it how destructive to reasonable expectations overblown Hollywood movies have always been. And how much I preferred the old Nora Ephron essays to the recent Nora Ephron films.)

Joan feels that a Holy Relationship is quite a different matter. Holy Relationships are *easy*. They don't require work because "we are not trying to *fit* the other person."

She opens a large drawing tablet and begins to draw a silhouette of a mountain. Simultaneously I begin to hear my own voice talking to me. Maybe it is my Guardian Angel. Maybe it is my Higher Self. I am not sure who it is but here is what it is saying: "I WANT SOUP."

Fortunately, Joan cannot hear this voice that screams so loudly within me, because she begins to explain her Iceberg Theory: That we live on the tip of an iceberg of unacknowledged, long-buried negative stuff that keeps us from accessing all the love at our core.

"Isn't this depressing?" she asks the group. "And you paid money to hear this?"

But I am not depressed. I am just increasingly obsessed with the idea of soup. It's the perfect thing. I am soo hungry. And as soon as class is over I will go in search of soup.

"You need to ask yourself, 'What do I *really want?*'" our teacher tells us. "Intimacy," says a very heavy guy with a green shirt whom I've seen at two other seminars. "Self-love," says a black woman in a multicolored coat and a long black scarf. "Peacefulness," says a sexually ambiguous Asian person with very long hair. "A thick soup, but not a cream soup," is what my inner voice is telling me. "Maybe something like a black bean soup or lentil."

I look over at my friend Judy to confer with her on my plans. She is going through the catalog in which I found this course, circling other courses that interest her. So far she has circled "How to Paint Furniture" and "Sailing."

People have been arriving throughout the lecture. An attractive black woman with a child of about five sleeping on her shoulder sits down right in front of us. I marvel at the way the child doesn't wake up during transit.

"How about the career of your dreams?" asks Joan of the class. "How about a healed relationship with your mother? Our greatest tool is forgiveness. Forgiveness offers everything. The holiest of all spots on earth is where an ancient betrayal becomes a present love."

"Betrayal has a baby," my inner voice says to me, "and that baby's name. . . . Minestrone." That's what I want. Minestrone. Perfect. At the Broadway Deli . . . it's a thick minestrone, and it comes with bread!

I would leave right now, but we are starting a forgiveness technique and everyone around me is settling into a peaceful meditative state. So we all close our eyes and begin to breathe deeply as we try to see ourselves not as we are today but as an enthusiastic young adult of twenty-two, then a seventeen year old full of dreams, then an awkward twelve year old. As I contemplate my twelve-year-old self, a brand new idea occurs to me: Split pea soup, which

I didn't like when I was twelve, but I sure do now. Especially the kind they have at that place on the Third Street mall. I am so pleased with this final decision that I am able to join the group and become an eight year old and then a little child of five and "a little toddler of two, such a precious, adorable little child. Love that little toddler. The heart of a little baby is like a little sponge waiting for water. Such an aura of peace."

It's all kind of lovely except the problem I am now having is . . . I'm getting drowsy. Soup is really the only answer. It will revive me and make me ready for Divine Love.

So I open my eyes to keep myself from dozing off entirely, and I find myself looking into the eyes of the little child lying on his mother's shoulder in front of me. He is staring right at me, head on its side, like a flounder.

"Be there in a moment of silence," says Joan, "with this wondrous baby that is you." She makes a dome shape with her hands. "Now before you is an enormous beautiful orb of white light. Release this infant into the light as a healing on every level begins to take place."

And almost as if on cue, the little child in front of me picks up his head and looks straight into my eyes. He is very peaceful. It all seems so perfect for a few seconds. Until he suddenly turns his head and looks to his right, and projectile-vomits onto the woman sitting beside him. It is a direct hit, even though she is seated a good six feet away.

I have never witnessed spontaneous projectile vomiting before, and I must say, it is every bit as spectacular as that scene in *The Exorcist*.

Immediately, his mother picks him up and takes him from the room, and a squadron of women with paper towels in hand appear. Cleanup progresses quickly all around me as Joan Gattuso, who probably missed most of the actual event because everyone doing the meditation had closed eyes, tries to incorporate what happened into her lecture. "Little children can always pick up a heavy vibe in a room," she says. If that's actually true, I'm not sure that she should be flattered. But I, for one, realize something else of *real* importance: Split pea soup is now out of the question.

But perhaps Divine Love works in mysterious ways and on many levels. Because very soon—within minutes after the meditation and the vomiting—I was able to enjoy the best bowl of minestrone I have had in fiscal '96. And I learned a valuable lesson: Sometimes a hot bowl of soup *is* as close to experiencing Divine Love as you are going to get.

Chapter 22
A Wrap-Up

SO HERE WE ARE AT THE END OF MY JOURNEY. AND LOOKING BACK, I feel I did learn some useful things.

I had always watched with exasperation and dismay the way love rendered reasonable, even smart women suddenly much stupider. One minute you have a friend who will discuss literature, current events, science. The next minute you are living in a real-life scene from *Invasion of the Body Snatchers* because someone seems to have replaced your nice, smart friend with an identical, much stupider look-alike.

Now she is calling six times a day saying, "Can I have your opinion on the answering machine message he just left me?" and "Okay, I just need to tell you this one other thing that he said."

I have not only watched these behaviors in others, I have lived these behaviors. And I have inflicted them on others. And I have always assumed that it was assorted nefarious and flaky childhood influences that caused a person in love to disintegrate into a poorly centered goofball.

Now I also understand that there is specific physiological chemistry that brings this behavior to a boil. That these inescapable chemical reactions, triggered by sex, are almost as profound a reason as the threat of sexually transmitted disease to include your brain on the list of organs that you consult when you're thinking of taking the plunge yet again. Even if you are a columnist who is facing a deadline and really, really need something to write about. Maybe especially then.

In the course of writing this book, I have also noticed that the greater the degree of craziness and obsession accompanying the relationship, the less the chance that it is headed for a happy ending. The more stable the love affair, the less the desire for constant discussion, analysis, and play-by-play by its participants. Particularly its female participants.

Nevertheless, the former condition can be so painful and confusing that it can serve a useful purpose if only as a reminder to single people to just shut up and count your blessings. And since it apparently takes at least three months for people in love to begin to reveal their true selves to each other, if you find yourself falling in love, you might as well just cross off the next twelve weeks on your calendar. Then inform all your friends that they should consider it an act of compassion that you may not be in touch with them for about ninety days. That way, should your love affair come apart, at least you will still have a few friends who can stand you.

Maybe one reason that love is such a messy area in our culture is that we are very low on reasonable role models to even pretend to emulate. Bill and Hillary, ha! Tipper and Al, yick. Once Paul Newman and Joanne Woodward are gone, I don't know what we're going to do. And I'm already dreading the tell-all book that is bound to turn up eventually, revealing the frightening details of what really was going on behind closed doors.

I personally am rooting for Pamela Anderson and Tommy Lee, just because I am a contrarian and the odds are *soo* against them. In fact, I wonder if anyone will remember that they were married by the time this book hits the stands.

Generally, the decline of love for any public couple can be charted from the first day they appear in *People* magazine, standing together in their fabulous newly renovated kitchen, feeding each other something from a very big spoon. If the article also contains the words "We're very much in love," you can confidently begin the office betting. The countdown to divorce has begun. By the time the telephoto lens shots begin to appear in the tabloids, it is just a matter of months, if not weeks.

And what have we learned from all the weird love we have watched ignite, blossom, and then disintegrate before our eyes on the public stage in recent years? Hmm. There must be something.

Okay, how about this: Roseanne and Tom Arnold taught us not to commingle our professional and married lives, not to share a PR person, and certainly not to commemorate any of the above with a tattoo.

Mia and Woody taught us that if you are *not* going to ever get married, then don't go ahead with the big family. Especially not adopted kids. Then again, Burt and Loni taught us that even the minimum definition of a married family can turn into a big mess in the hands of out-of-control, narcissistically disordered show business personalities. Perhaps one day, in a more just world, they will all simply be forbidden to marry and to breed, let alone adopt. After all, society ends up paying the price by having to watch the terrible movie efforts of their needy screwed-up offspring.

I guess from Liz and Larry Fortensky we learn not to select our mates from the mixer at the rehab facility. This is a particularly hard lesson for those of us in Los Angeles since that's where all the cute guys hang out. To be fair, Liz probably thought she was taking an important developmental step by not going for yet another high-profile, flamboyant, famous guy. But sadly for her, in this case someone with no particular visible appeal was still just not enough.

From Michael Jackson and Lisa Marie we learn that it's not a good idea to marry someone who has had more plastic surgery than you. Come to think of it, we have learned that from every couple I've mentioned.

For the life of me, I don't know what we learned from Charles and Di. Perhaps to be grateful that most of us will never be faced with the temptation of dating a member of the royal family. Actually, maybe "temptation" is overstating the case.

And ultimately, it appears that, as much as we learn about love, there is still more we do not understand. Should love be all accepting? Once again I quote an anonymous Hallmark poet, who wrote:

All the time
No matter how I'm acting
on the outside
I'm loving you
on the inside.

Of course, that's the approach O. J. Simpson used, and we all know how that turned out. That Hallmark now makes a card to meet the greeting needs of the psychopath is certainly a step in some direction. Which direction is not completely clear.

Looking back through the chapters of my book, here are the other things I have learned:

1. If tomatoes were *ever* called love apples, they certainly haven't been in a very long time.
2. Retaining semen through testicle breathing loosens the skull.
3. Women produce fifty times more oxytocin, a chemical that creates a feeling of bonding from the sex act, than do men.
4. The difference between being in love and having an allergy to eggs is that if you have an allergy to eggs you are not as likely to be arrested for stalking.
5. Flirtatious eye contact lasts two seconds longer than casual eye contact.
6. Kiwi, pineapple, and celery make semen taste sweeter. Asparagus and garlic make it taste bitter.

7. Don't forget the stepchildren.

8. Oven mitts are restrictive and clumsy, but that's what makes them fun. Both you and your lover can wear them while you make love.

9. Men, please do call a woman the next day after sex even if you never want to see her again. Just say something like, "I really liked jumping your bones and I'll call you later."

10. One of the hardest things for anyone to watch is a grown man crying. After a woman rejects you, put your head in your hands and quietly start to sob.

11. Flushing a chick down the toilet of humiliation is almost as great a kick as scoring.

12. Think carefully before you establish a relationship with a deceased person. You do not want to get involved with a succubus or an incubus.

13. Betrayal has a baby, and that baby's name is bitterness.

14. Remember to clean the clocks off the fireplace of your heart.

15. Processes by which singles meet are: introductions, matchmakers, and while out with friends.

16. Giving is masculine. Giving *back* is feminine.

17. Featherweight Lenscrafters are so strong that you can back over them with your car.

18. Everyone should have an Italian at least once.

19. The less you know about the object of your affection, the better it is for the future of your romance.

20. A Holy Relationship requires no work because you are not trying to *fit* the other person.

21. Sometimes a bowl of minestrone is as close to Divine Love as you are going to get.

22. Love *is* a Dimpling Doodle Bug, after all.